To

DEFINING THE CALL

Thanks for your support!

www.selfpublishn30days.com

Published by *Self Publish -N- 30 Days*

Copyright 2019 Defining The Call.

All rights reserved worldwide. No part of this book may be reproduced or transmitted in any form or by any means electronic or mechanical, including photocopying, recording or by any information storage and retrieval system without written permission from Daniel Krebs or Action Shift Co.

Printed in the United States of America

ISBN: 978-1098763961

1. Ministry 2. Leadership

Daniel Krebs: Defining The Call.

Defining The Call

Disclaimer/Warning:

This book is intended for lecture and entertainment purposes only. The author or publisher does not guarantee that anyone following these steps will be successful in ministry. The author and publisher shall have neither liability responsibility to anyone with respect to any loss or damage cause, or alleged to be caused, directly or indirectly by the information contained in this book.

Unless otherwise noted, Scriptures are taken from the
Holy Bible, New International Version (NIV)

DEDICATION

To my wife and partner, Lenise, who has stood with me through some amazing times in ministry, memories that are still being written. Your prayers and support is what has sustained and challenged me to always aim for higher in all that God has for us. Without you, this journey and this book would not have been possible to achieve.

> *"... she is worth far more than rubies that make one rich.*
> *The heart of her husband trusts in her,*
> *and he will never stop getting good things."*
> **Proverbs 31:10b-11**

To my children, Taylor, Jordan and Aliyah, I am honored to be called your father. Although it hasn't always been easy carrying the title of "Pastor's Kids," you wore it well and I am so proud of the adults you have become.

> *"Children are a gift from the Lord.*
> *The children born to us are our special reward."*
> **Psalm 127:3**

To contact Daniel Krebs for teaching or speaking engagements, email him at

contact.danielkrebs@gmail.com

or visit his website at www.danielkrebs.net

Table of Contents

Introduction		1
Chapter 1	"Trying" Ministry	5
Chapter 2	Before You Were Born, I Set You Apart	17
Chapter 3	Square Pegs in Round Holes	31
Chapter 4	Distinct Callings in Crucial Times	37
Chapter 5	The Calling of Joseph	41
Chapter 6	The Calling of Moses	81
Chapter 7	The Calling of David	129
Chapter 8	Don't Forget Your First Love	177
Conclusion		183

INTRODUCTION

Defining a divine call to ministry from God is like trying to define a feeling or an experience. How does one describe or explain something that they supernaturally feel inside? You could try to use word pictures and illustrations to try to explain how a calling actually feels to you, yet in the end, most that don't have one, will never be able to fully grasp it.

I compare it to a sport like scuba diving. Twenty-seven years ago, during my honeymoon in the Dominican Republic with my new bride, Lenise, I decided to take one of those one-day courses so I could scuba dive in the Caribbean waters. Looking back, and now having my open waters license after proper training, I can clearly see that a one-day course was probably not exactly one of the wisest moves that I made in my life. The rushed training can really put an inexperienced person at risk and one wrong move could have put a real damper on one's holidays!

Even a three-hour class doesn't exactly go into much depth of all the dangers involved in the sport. Nevertheless, the next day, there I was at 30 feet below the surface and experiencing colors of fish and coral that I had, up unto that point, only seen in pictures and videos. Nothing could have prepared me for this incredible moment.

Wow! I couldn't wait to get back to the surface and tell my new bride how amazing the whole experience was. Yet for some reason, Lenise didn't seem to express the same enthusiasm and excitement that I had. She tried to do her best by snorkeling on the surface, but couldn't get past the idea of breathing under water. Trying this quickly caused her to have a panic attack which ended any attempt on her part to try a new adventure like scuba diving, or in her case, snorkeling! Within seconds, Lenise was safely back on the boat, waiting for me to finally get this experience out of my system.

Climbing back on the boat, I could instantly see that Lenise wasn't having the same euphoric experience that I was. I tried to relay to her the incredible beauty this new underwater world had to offer, yet I quickly realized that my descriptions were futile. Unless the other person has experienced it for themselves, or at least had a passion for that type of thing, trying to explain it and get their interest would most likely result in a gazed, empty stare looking back at you.

Then there was the time I decided to go skydiving while Lenise stayed on the ground watching me jump out of a plane at 3,500 feet! Well, no need to go there. I think you get the idea.

For me to try to explain the calling on my life to others is like trying to explain my experience and thrill of scuba diving or skydiving to my lovely young bride. If it's not in you, you probably won't understand it. It's not something that one can always explain, and it is definitely not something that easily makes sense.

Jesus says in Matthew 22:14 (KJV), when He was giving the parable of the banquet, "For many are called but few are chosen." Without taking this verse too far out of context, when it comes to the calling to ministry, there needs to be an understanding that, in one sense, all of us who consider ourselves believers in Christ and desire to follow Him in every aspect of our lives, are technically "called." Yet, there is no denying the fact that there are also those who have been chosen by the Lord for a uniquely different life.

In defining the aspect of one's calling, I will be quite transparent about my own journey as I personally wrestled with this concept of being called from a young age. I did not fully understand what this meant and had no idea what was demanded or required of me.

In these pages, we will discuss how the calling has times of incredible rewards, moments of euphoria and seasons of excitement and miracles. Yet, in some of those same moments, you will quickly experience times of unimaginable pain, loneliness, and life-altering experiences that will challenge your faith and change your life forever.

Despite the difficulties, you will discover that it is these same moments, these same obstacles, that will help shape you into the leader God desires you to be, no matter what direction your calling may take you.

We will be confronting some of the typical stereotypes of being called into ministry. Fallacies abound, such as everyone can be called to ministry, as well as the myth that a called individual looks at working for the Lord like every other believer.

We will delve into the lives of three patriarchs of the Older Testament, Joseph, Moses and David, who all had very distinct callings and at very crucial times in biblical history. In doing so, we will uncover interesting aspects of their lineages, their lessons and their legacies.

In their lineages, we examine a bit of their family trees and some of the passed down character traits that these men possessed which enabled them to be the leaders that God called them to be. We'll see how these traits are also some of the same qualities that each called person will need to have, or at least learn to develop, in order to reach their greatest potential in their divine calling.

We will discover the lessons that each patriarch had to learn. Lessons that, through the school of hard knocks, helped them refine their areas of weakness. We will be able to identify with those lessons and understand that each called individual will also need to learn these lessons as well.

In looking at these men's legacies, we will see how their impact left their fingerprint on the world. This will challenge each called man or woman to ask the same question. What type of legacy do you desire to leave?

In the last chapter, "Don't Forget Your First Love," I will discuss briefly the importance of never forgetting your first love when it comes to why God called you in the first place. This chapter would be more for the man or woman of God in ministry that might have a few miles behind them. This will challenge you to re-evaluate where your ministry has brought you and perhaps encourage a little soul-searching to explore the idea that perhaps there are other doors of ministry yet to be considered.

As you read these pages, it is my prayer that you will come to a deeper understanding and appreciation of what the calling means. If you are coming to grips with considering that perhaps God has placed a special calling on your life, I pray that you would not fear it, nor curse it, but rather embrace it and by faith walk into it.

If someone reading these pages knows of someone who feels that they have a calling from the Lord and you are trying to understand what this means, I pray that this book will help you appreciate what your friend or loved one is going through. I pray that you will be a catalyst who God uses to help your loved one reach their greatest potential in God's calling for their future.

Daniel Krebs

CHAPTER 1

"TRYING" MINISTRY
(YOU MAY WANT TO RETHINK THAT IDEA)

"So, when did you decide to go into ministry?" If only I had a nickel for every time someone asked me that question. I've lost track of how many times I have had conversations with individuals, usually young people, who were trying to figure out what God's will was for their lives. "Maybe I should try ministry. It looks like a cool job," responding as if they were looking over a job advertisement on some online or newspaper job posting sight.

Without trying to sound too sarcastic, I would always stress, "If you are not called, don't even consider ministry."

My response was never to scare or deter them from a calling that the Lord may be instilling in their hearts, but rather to resist the urge of just "trying" ministry because it was something that they thought was cool or was encouraged by their pastor, parents or a loved one.

More than once I have heard someone tell me that they went off to Bible school because their parents thought it would be good for them. Then, once graduated, they felt compelled to try ministry because, "Hey, I paid for it," only to find out that once in the trenches of ministry work, they hated every minute of it.

DEFINING THE CALL

James 3:1 says, "Not many of you should become teachers, my fellow believers, because you know that we who teach will be judged more strictly." This verse, of course, could also include other facets and avenues of ministry and would be just as accurate.

Those who have a calling to spiritual leadership need to understand that they will be judged differently than others. Therefore, one needs to be completely convinced that this is what they have been called to before they take up this mantle.

I'm sure you've heard of the incredible trends that are going on right now with North American pastors. Many are leaving by the droves. They are running for the hills, saying that they would rather pump gas than ever minister in a church again.

Although I completely understand the stresses of the ministry, I do believe that there are many pastors and leaders who started out with great intentions, and perhaps with some natural ability. Yet, because it wasn't their real calling, their drive and passion quickly fizzled out. As John Maxwell puts it, "Burnout is NOT doing too much of something, burnout is doing any amount of the wrong thing."

Obviously, I am not saying that this is the case for all pastors and church leaders who have burned out at some point in their ministry. What I am suggesting is that is it possible that one reason for the increased defections from ministry today is due to the fact that many of these people were not even called to that work in the first place. Perhaps it was never explained clearly enough what they were getting themselves into and how it would affect their lives.

To be quite frank, if you're not sure if you are called or not, do everything to resist it! Seriously, I mean this. Entering into the Lord's work on a semi or full-time basis should never be taken lightly. Far too many who have tried it have quickly found out how much of a mistake it was.

Yet, if you have continually sought the Lord about the calling and it still keeps nagging and tugging at your soul, no matter how hard you've tried to beat it down, then maybe, just maybe, you might have a calling on your life.

ALL IN OR ALL OUT

The idea of trying ministry drives me almost as crazy as those who say, "Try Jesus." Never in Scripture do we ever read Jesus saying to those who were curious about following Him, "Listen, just try me. If it doesn't work out, hey at least you tried."

The idea of trying Jesus almost gives the impression that there are other options. As if He is "door number three" on a spiritual game show of Let's Make a Deal, or like a blindfold taste test between Pepsi and Coke.

Jesus was always very clear in His call to salvation. "Whoever wants to be my disciple must deny themselves and take up their cross daily and follow me" (Luke 9:23). There is nothing in the Bible about trying Jesus. There is nothing there about this Christian life being easy. Jesus was always making it very clear, saying that you better count the cost before coming to Him.

In Luke 14:28, Jesus uses the illustration of a builder who decided to build a tower. He says:

"Suppose one of you wants to build a tower. Won't you first sit down and estimate the cost to see if you have enough money to complete it? For if you lay the foundation and are not able to finish it, everyone who sees it will ridicule you, saying, 'This person began to build and wasn't able to finish.'"

Many individuals who start out serving the Lord, and were never challenged about what this decision may cost them, end up abandoning their faith, only to feel embarrassed and determined never to dart the doors of the church again.

In Luke 9:58, Jesus replied, "Foxes have dens and birds have nests, but the Son of Man has no place to lay his head." Jesus did everything to deter people from following Him for the wrong motives.

Unfortunately, many of our churches, with great intentions, have lost or have tried to redefine the meaning of a sold out commitment to the Lord in order to make it more palatable for their congregants. Because of this, they have lost what this incredible, powerful, life-altering message has to offer!

Jesus said that no man can come to Him, unless the Father draws him (John 6:44). The call to ministry has the same perspective. If you are called, it's because He chose you and will give you the spiritual tools and abilities to be used this way.

In Jeremiah 1:5, the Lord says to this man of God, "Before I formed you in the womb I knew you, before you were born I set you apart." Jeremiah was "set apart" and called to a very specific and very difficult task of being God's messenger to God's rebellious people, Israel.

One who is called in this manner is not given this mandate because they had all the natural abilities to do so. In fact, the majority of the men and women who have a calling do so with an overwhelming sense of being inferior and unqualified for the task.

Even Jeremiah showed his state of mind in receiving his call by crying out to the Lord immediately, in verse 6, saying, "Alas, Sovereign Lord, I do not know how to speak: I am too young."

In the John Maxwell Leaders Bible, the commentary on Jeremiah 1 about being called says, "If God calls you, heed the call. He will also give you the resources to accomplish the work. But if He hasn't called you, don't conjure up some self-appointment. If He doesn't send you, you will not ultimately succeed."

ALL ARE CHOSEN TO DO SOMETHING

Some of you reading this might be thinking, "What do you mean God chose you? Are you telling me that you didn't have a say in God's plan for your life?" Well, without getting into much discussion about eternal security, free-will and election, I do want to touch on the reality of the incredible divine ordination that God has placed upon all of us as His children, whether called into ministry or not.

I knew that when I thought about writing this book that even suggesting that some followers of Christ are set apart for a deeper calling to ministry could cause some to think that God shows favoritism. Yet the fact remains, as mentioned above, that Jesus tells us in John 15:16, "You did not choose me, but I chose you and appointed you to go and bear fruit – fruit that will last." If we consider ourselves a follower of Christ, God has an incredible plan to use our lives (whether we are called to ministry or not). His goal for each and every one of us is to "bear fruit – fruit that will last," no matter what direction the Lord leads our lives.

When recently cleaning out the shed in our backyard, I decided to pull out an old hope chest that had not seen the light of day in over 15 years. Before opening it, I decided to call my wife and three kids (young adults, actually) over to enjoy the "time capsule" moment with me. Well, we were not disappointed when we discovered all kinds of things that we haven't seen in a very long time.

There were things like Lenise's wedding dress, which both my daughters tried on, and my college school jacket, which was so small that even my 6-foot son wasn't able to fit in it. I didn't realize I had been so scrawny. We found love letters and cards that I wrote to Lenise when we were dating and some of our kids' school projects when they were only 5-7 years of age.

When I finally removed all of these items, right there at the bottom of the box were about 10 of my favorite albums that I thought I had lost decades ago, including four albums from the late Keith Green. Man, I loved his music! It affected my spiritual walk in so many ways and seeing those records again caused so many memories to rush back into my mind. To this very day, I find myself singing his songs from time to time, remembering every word, and feeling that same powerful conviction in my spirit.

In some of the songs that he wrote, Keith was very vocal in stating his belief that all believers were called to go into world missions. In the early years of Keith's faith, his incredible passion for world evangelism was such that he whole-heartedly believed that if all followers of Christ would take our faith more seriously, we would all be boarding the first plane to some far-off country to preach to the unreached people groups of the world.

Since I felt a calling on my life to some sort of ministry, this seemed perfectly logical and made perfect sense to me. Because of this, I could not understand why many of my Christian peers didn't have that same passion for a more in-depth, full-time Christian work for themselves.

It was only when I was in seminary that I began to understand and appreciate that each of us have very different and unique callings that have been predestined by God himself.

In Paul's first letter to the Corinthian church, he spends several chapters dealing with the moving of the Holy Spirit and the gifts that accompany those who believe. In 1 Corinthians 12:7-11, he writes:

"Now to each one the manifestation of the Spirit is given for the common good. To one there is given through the Spirit a message of wisdom, to another a message of knowledge by means of the same Spirit, to another faith by the same Spirit, to another gifts of healing by that one Spirit, to another miraculous powers, to another prophecy, to another distinguishing between spirits, to another speaking in different kinds of tongues and to still another the interpretation of tongues. All these are the work of one and the same Spirit, and He distributes them to each one, just as He determines."

These gifts that Paul mentions could very easily be perceived as being gifts for those in clerical ministry. He speaks about things like wisdom, knowledge, faith, healing, miraculous powers and so on. Each and every one of these gifts could (and should) also be used in the marketplaces of our society.

I'm sure we could all agree that our secular colleges and universities, many of which have strong left leanings and socialistic political world views, need some godly, biblically-based professors and teachers on campus. I'm sure you would agree that our politically correct, egocentric, and ethically challenged society could use a few more believers in key areas of influence to help stem the tide of North America's moral erosion.

Paul again speaks about spiritual gifts in his letter to the Romans at 12:4-8, he writes:

"For just as each of us has one body with many members, and these members do not all have the same function, so in Christ we, though many, form one body, and each member belongs to all the others. We have different gifts, according to the grace given to each of us. If your gift is prophesying, then prophesy in accordance with your faith; if it is serving, then serve; if it is teaching, then teach; if it is to encourage, then give encouragement; if it is giving, then give generously; if it is to lead, do it diligently; if it is to show mercy, do it cheerfully."

To continue with Paul's explanation to the believers on the importance of all being chosen to do something, we see his connection of the physical body of a believer and the spiritual body of all believers, called the Church.

To the Church at Corinth, Paul dramatizes his illustration by saying in 1 Corinthians 12:15-16:

"Now if the foot should say, 'Because I am not a hand, I do not belong to the body,' it would not for that reason stop being part of the body. And if the ear should say, 'Because I am not an eye, I do not belong to the body,' it would not for that reason stop being part of the body."

We see this same likeness from Paul when he says in Romans 12:4-5:

"For just as each of us has one body with many members, and these members do not all have the same function, so in Christ we, though many, form one body, and each member belongs to all the others."

Every person has been called by the Holy Spirit to serve the Lord and plays a very important role in God's Kingdom and the Body of Christ. I have found that some of the most amazing people who had the gift of generosity, as mentioned in Romans 12:8, are not in clerical ministry.

Rather, they lead very successful lives in business. Many of which started out with nothing, but because of their God-given business sense, have thrived and have used their blessings to bless others.

I have also found that some of the most amazing people who have been given the gift of encouragement, as found in Romans 12:7, may actually be driving a city transit bus, a taxi, or even working in clinics, hospitals and senior homes. They are using their gift of encouragement in ways that no full-time Christian counselor or evangelist could ever do with the same results.

I think that it is a major problem with the church today that we have left the role of evangelism to the evangelists and pastors. The thinking is, "After all, isn't that what we pay them for?" Because of this attitude, the church has become irrelevant in the marketplace. Believers in the marketplace are no longer being an influence in this post Judeo-Christian secular environment.

ALL HAVE GIFTS TO USE!

When it comes to evangelism, all believers and followers of Christ are responsible to reach their world for Jesus! Yet, as Paul makes it clear in Ephesians 4:11 (NASB, emphasis added), "He gave SOME as Apostles, and SOME as prophets, and SOME as evangelists and SOME as pastors and teachers." Therefore, we can see that within the church, God has equipped each of us with unique gifts and abilities.

When it comes to reaching our world for Jesus, we have all been conscripted into His spiritual army and He wants to use each and every one of us in the gifts of the Spirit that make this challenge of world evangelism possible.

It has never been the responsibility of only those individuals who work in ministry to do the work. Every one of us is equipped for something and God desires to use all believers in these gifts. In fact, I would argue that the majority of the work of the Holy Spirit happens, or needs to happen, outside of the church through the lives of everyday people. How can we be a light in our ever-increasing secularized culture without being involved and connected in all the major facets of our society?

Each part of the body plays an intricate part in God's plan for global evangelism. Paul continues illustrating the body when he says in 1 Corinthians 12:23b-24:

"The parts that we think are less honorable we treat with special honor. And the parts that are unpresentable are treated with special modesty while our presentable parts need no special treatment. But God has put the body together, giving greater honor to the parts that lacked it."

When I read these words from Paul, I like to think that the less honorable or less seen parts of the body of Christ represent those who work in the shadows of God's Kingdom, those who nobody notices, but in the end, everyone appreciates.

Let us never get caught up with the hierarchical attitude that James and John had, wondering who would be seated on Jesus' left and right in His Kingdom. God has predestined all of us to different types of work. And the fact is, there are some who will be receiving incredible rewards in heaven who were never even recognized by others while living in this world.

The only reason why the widow in Mark 12 and Luke 21 is mentioned for giving her last coin to the Lord is because Jesus Himself was the one who pointed her out. If Jesus never gave the comparison between her and the Pharisees' behavior, she would have faded into history without anyone even taking notice. Anyone that is, except Jesus. He saw her then, and He knew of all her noble deeds done in secret, prior to and after this recorded incident at the temple.

We're not given the names of the 70 sent ones who went out and evangelized their region for Jesus, but we are told about this widow individually. Oh, maybe not by name, but rather by deed. And in my imagination, I like to creatively think that maybe she became one of those saints who filled one of those two seats in God's kingdom that James and John were so hoping to have dibs on.

In Romans 8:29a, the Apostle Paul writes, "For those God foreknew he also predestined to be conformed to the image of his Son."

As children of God, we have all been predestined for two goals: to conform to the image of Jesus and to do our best to fulfill His desired will in our lives. Whatever task is placed before us, we are responsible to commit ourselves to that task. By whole-heartedly doing so, we eventually conform to His likeness.

This widow, despite her poverty and reclusiveness, fulfilled her duty in giving what was required of her by God, which was everything. To others, her sacrifice seemed minuscule and useless. Yet to Jesus, she became a mirror image of God's character by being obedient down to her last penny.

God is an infinite, all-knowing God. Therefore, we cannot, and will never in this life, ever be able to claim to understand the plans that He laid out for our personal lives. Because of this, we will many times question why some believers seem to get all the blessings while others seem to be left feeding on the crumbs.

There is a reason why the Lord compares us to children and to sheep. We are His children because we will never be able to comprehend the complexity of God's decisions, and we are His sheep because we are called to just obey and follow our good shepherd in whatever direction He may have for us.

When my kids were younger, they could not comprehend why they were forced to live under the rules of their loving parents. Going to bed on time, brushing their teeth and eating their vegetables seemed to be such needless, unnecessary tasks that made no sense to their undeveloped minds.

As God's children, our finite minds can never truly understand the complexities of His ultimate plan for us and for the world. That is why we are called to "walk by faith, not by sight" (2 Corinthians 5:7).

As we read in Romans 9:20-21, Paul deals with this seemingly unfair fact of predestination when he says:

"But who are you, a human being, to talk back to God? "Shall what is formed say to the one who formed it, 'Why did you make me like this?'" Does not the potter have the right to make out of the same lump of clay some pottery for special purposes and some for common use?"

Paul is saying that rather than trying to figure God out as to why our lives have been dealt the cards that they have, we must accept the roadmap that He has set out for us. We have no right to talk back to God.

For He is the potter and we are the clay. We are never called to try to obtain the "cards" that God has dealt to someone else's life, but rather take what we have been dealt and use it to its greatest potential.

CHAPTER 2

BEFORE YOU WERE BORN, I SET YOU APART

In the last chapter we spoke about how God desires to use each and every one of us in the gifts of the Spirit. Whether we are called to ministry or not, there are gifts that God wants all of us to use to change our world. As I already alluded to in the previous pages, the majority of these gifts are most effective in the secular environment in direct contact with the everyday world.

But, if you have been reading this book up to this point and your commitment to ministry is at least still curious, then I would encourage you to read on.

Ministry has the ability to damage you emotionally and even spiritually unless the Lord has prepared you for it. Your natural abilities will only take you so far and your degrees and diplomas will only bring you to a certain level.

What will keep you going in the calling and what will prepare you for the challenges of ministry that lie ahead is what has been birthed in you by God Himself. It is He who will cultivate and fertilize that seed, and it is only through the Lord's permitted challenges and pains of life that you will become the spiritual leader that God sees in you.

The pain and tests that will come your way, along with your spiritual stubbornness, will twist and bend you into the mighty oak that He created you to be. The amazing thing is that the torments and attacks that the devil himself throws at you to try to stop you from following the call on your life are the very same painful experiences that, in a miraculous way, God uses to mold and transform you into the vessel you need to be. For, "what the devil meant for evil, God will use for good" (Genesis 50:20).

One needs to understand that if God is calling you, the Lord will begin to prepare you early on in life. As mentioned earlier, Jeremiah had an incredible revelation of his own calling when the Lord tells him; "Before I formed you in the womb, I knew you, before you were born, I set you apart; I appointed you as a prophet to the nations."

God's plan for him, and for all of us for that matter, was set in place even before our conception. Whether it was Moses, Joseph, David, or any of the patriarchs in the Scriptures, when you read their stories, you always see that God started the process for their future calling the instant they were born, whether they realized it or not.

There is no time for easy living; there is no time to be just like everyone else. God's time of preparation for the called begins long before we are even aware of the calling. Perhaps it was long before you even believed in God, let alone understood that He had a plan for you to follow.

In my own life, I can see that the preparation was happening long before I could comprehend that God even loved me, let alone had a calling for me. I understand now that the trials I faced were the testing ground for God to prepare me for something bigger.

Family therapy pioneer and author, Virginia Satir, said the following, "Life is not the way it's supposed to be, it's the way it is. The way you cope with it is what makes the difference."

In his book, The 15 Invaluable Laws of Growth, John Maxwell states in his chapter, The Law of Pain, "The good management of bad experiences leads to great growth and is necessary to grow."

God want us to manage our bad experiences well, to learn from them, and to grow from them. As a pastor, many times I told my congregations, "When you are going through difficult times, stop asking God 'why' and begin to ask God 'how!'"

"How Lord? How will you use this difficulty to use me more effectively, more successfully?" You may not get the answer immediately. I would be surprised if you did. But, it will help you change your focus to be more on your future blessings rather than your present sufferings. This is what will transform you in becoming the victor that God wants you to be rather than the victim.

To be called to ministry requires a spiritual depth and perspective of life that can only be fostered and developed through trial and pain. There is no other remedy that can accomplish this. Pain and challenges are the fertilizer that enriches one's character in preparing you for what lies ahead in your calling.

TWO CHILDHOODS

When I look back upon my early years, it's almost as if I had two childhoods. One was filled with blue skies, bell-bottom pants, the Brady Bunch, days at the beach and camping trips. In the other childhood, I see damp cloudy days, isolation, deep depression and a fear of the unknown.

The first childhood were my years in Kitchener, Ontario, Canada, where I was born in 1966. Kitchener was my hometown for 10 years, until my father moved his young family to Thunder Bay, Ontario, Canada in 1977.

Now, I understand that many times as a young child, especially the early years, one's memories may be skewed due to childish innocence, but I've got to tell you, life just seemed to make so much more sense overall at this time in my life.

Being so close to the U.S./Canadian border, our family spent each summer visiting our cousins in either Michigan or in New York State. We had a great house, lived in a nice neighborhood, and, as a child, although my dad had his issues (to say the least), living in Kitchener just seemed right. Hey, even Elvis was still alive!

This, of course, was from the eyes of a child. I was too young to understand the stresses that my family was going through and I definitely had no idea of the storm that awaited us on the horizon.

As a child of immigrant parents from Germany, I always felt that the Krebs' were a bit different than the other "normal" Canadian families on our street.

My father was a strong disciplinarian and I often wondered why he couldn't be more enjoyable and fun to be around like the other dads. As children, a nervous tension was never far from our minds. We loved Dad, but there was this incredible fear of him as well.

As time went on, his outbursts of anger and verbal and physical abuse seemed to grow stronger and more violent and frequent. This caused us kids to begin to blame ourselves for not being good enough for our father's love. He had a staunch German disciplinarian attitude and lived by the old world adage that a child *"should be seen and not heard."*

On the outside, Dad was what many Christians would call a good, moral father and husband. Standing out in a crowd at 6'4", Gerhard Krebs and his tall blonde haired children weren't easy to miss either. Leading the church choir and being a Sunday school teacher and church board member, it looked like Gerhard Krebs had the perfect church family. However, on the inside, it did not look the same. None of us as a family, including Mom, understood what Dad was dealing with emotionally.

In 1976, Dad's restlessness got the best of him and he told my mother that he was pursuing a job in Thunder Bay, Ontario. As a child, all I can recall is Dad being gone for months. He was working in Thunder Bay, while at the same time preparing the new home that we were going to live in so that his young family could once and for all join him in his latest adventure.

So, in 1977, we found ourselves moving all the way to Northern Ontario to Thunder Bay. It felt to us kids that this city was in the middle of nowhere. There were no friends or family nearby and everything that we were used to was over 2,000 miles away. To us kids, that kind of distance made it seem like we moved to the other side of the world.

Living in Kitchener, we were close to our friends and family. My oldest two sisters were in their senior years of high school, and we were well established in our local church.

To have made this kind of move, especially for my sisters having to attend a new school at this late stage of high school, and to deal with all these changes, was incredibly difficult for us kids, especially for them.

Compared to Southern Ontario, Thunder Bay took some getting used to, but it did have some benefits. In fact, it was while in Thunder Bay that I took up downhill skiing, learned to appreciate the art of hunting and enjoying the outdoors, graduated from high school, had my first kiss, my first car, and got my first dog, whom we named "Nikki."

Over the next three years of our family living in Thunder Bay, Dad's moods began to alter significantly. When you are only in the pre-teen years of 11 and 12, like I was at the time, you really don't have the maturity to understand what is going on. But looking back now, I can say that Dad's mood swings began to get more and more unpredictable and violent.

When he would come home from work, you were never quite sure who was going to come though those doors. I remember moments when all of us kids would be sitting in the living room after school and we would see Dad pulling up in our green station wagon. There were always these moments of fear and uncertainty.

Whatever the cause of his anger, Dad's physical outbursts began to play havoc on the entire family on a more daily basis. My sisters handled it in their own way and I became more and more reclusive. I was filled with fear and incredible anger toward my father and perhaps even toward God.

In 1980, the company that my father worked for went on strike. Rather than supporting the union, my father chose to take on a temporary job in Montreal, Quebec at Bonbardier Aerospace. While he was away, I can remember actually enjoying his absence. I missed the fact that my dad was not around, but man, did I enjoy not having to fear the unknown.

I'll never forget the date of May 30, 1980. It was a cold, rainy, damp and dreary afternoon. The four of us kids were in the basement of the house watching an after-school movie on the television. The phone rang, and my sister Monica, who was sixteen at the time, went upstairs to answer it.

A few minutes later, I remember her coming back down and saying with a blank look on her face, "That was the Montreal police who said that Dad is dead." I can remember so clearly how I responded. All three of my sisters started to cry uncontrollably and I just sat there looking at them. I tried to cry, and even let out a whimper, but I remember thinking, "Why can't I cry?" I wanted to, but I think I was in too much shock to even respond with tears.

To this day, I don't understand why the police notified our family of Dad's death this way. We were all children, and now as a father of three young adults myself, I can't imagine them going through what my sisters and I had to go through that May afternoon.

After that phone call, we all went upstairs and sat on the front porch of the house in the rain, waiting for Mom to come home from work. We were in shock and were trying to convince ourselves that perhaps it was a prank phone call or maybe a wrong number. But deep down inside, we all knew that it was the truth.

It was at that moment that Mom pulled up in the driveway. She told us years later, "I was wondering why you kids were all sitting out in the rain on the front porch. It looked so strange."

I'll never forget our mother's reaction when we broke the news. She broke down in a way that I never saw before. She was inconsolable. I remember thinking that my mom will never be the same again and there is nothing I can do to help her.

Frantic phone calls were made to see if the news was true. Once things were verified, it felt like all hell broke loose in our home. Suddenly our home was filled with people consoling our family. Every few minutes the doorbell would ring with another person, a neighbor, a co-worker, a church member, the pastor, all coming to comfort my mom and her four children.

Phone calls from our relatives in the States were coming in non-stop and each time, explanations had to be repeated over and over again as to what happened to Dad. Truth was, none of us really knew what happened to him. We had no information and only knew days later that he was found dead in his hotel room.

While all this craziness was going on, I can honestly say that I never had such opposing feelings in my heart at the same time. Part of me was incredibly sad to know that my father was dead. Another part of me felt incredibly guilty because I had prayed so many times that he would die. And yet, another part of me was at peace knowing that Dad wouldn't be there anymore to slap us around.

As a 13 year-old boy, I certainly did not understand what was happening within me and I felt terribly confused for having all of these opposing feelings.

As weeks turned into months, the official report of my father's death was that it remained inconclusive. It was quite likely a suicide, and yet they said they couldn't rule out foul play either. Because of this, the mortgage insurance company agreed to pay for our home. This was an incredible miracle, since it was in their policy that mortgage insurance doesn't cover suicide.

Since my father carried no life insurance, having our house paid for was a wonderful blessing that allowed us to stay in our home. Despite this blessing, the moment my father died, we went from being a typical middle-class family to overnight being a family where money was extremely tight.

As a family member of a possible suicide, you find that your identity completely changes. Your family is suddenly stigmatized as dysfunctional and broken. Those haunting questions that people wanted to know, how my dad died so young, if he had been sick or if it was an accident, were continually being asked those early years following his death. I never really knew how to answer. I hated being looked at as less-than and different from other families and I was convinced that my life would never be "normal" ever again.

It was at this time in my life that I began to feel that I didn't have much time for God. I felt He was cruel when Dad was around and causing so much fear in our home. Now that Dad was gone, God's cruelty was proven even further for allowing us to go through all this garbage.

I watched my mom struggling to keep our family together. She worked a full-time job as a homemaker where she took care of the elderly in order to make ends meet. Most days I came home from school to an empty house and the only one to meet me in the doorway was my dog, Nikki.

Now give me a second to talk about my dog. Nikki was a pet that I spent more money on as a child than I care to remember. As a kid, one job that I had was a paper route and I'm sure every penny that I made went into owning that animal. Whether it was when he was on the losing end of a porcupine or the time he came home with a bullet hole in his paw, Nikki was one wild Huskie that refused to be trained.

Yet despite his shortfalls, I always felt that this dog was the one true friend that helped me keep my sanity in those difficult years, especially after my dad died. I always joked with my three sisters and my mom that Nikki was the only other male in the family and he helped me through a lot.

There were many times that I took long walks through the woods with him or rather I should say *he* walked me. It was these special moments that I have very fond memories of talking with God in a very intimate, childlike and personal way that helped me stay focused. It's amazing when you look back and can see how the Lord could use even something like your pet dog to help you get through some of your darkest times.

I began to develop a very morbid perspective of myself. By this time, I was pretty well convinced in my heart that I wouldn't live much longer. I thought suicide was in my blood. Not only did my dad take his life, but my grandfather hung himself as well when my father was only a boy in Germany during the war.

What hope did I have to live a full life? I felt that I was dealt the same hand of cards as the two generations before me, and there was no real reason to plan for the future. If both my grandfather and dad felt that they couldn't make it themselves, why in the world should I kid myself into thinking that I was any different?

I had no male role models in my life to look up to, and because Dad chose to move us all the way up to Northern Ontario, I had no relatives that lived nearby that I could call on. I never felt so helpless in my entire life.

During the immediate years following my dad's death, my emotional wellbeing began to be more and more dark and desperate. I began to struggle greatly in school and I was failing everything.

I remember the day there was a knock on the door of my classroom. I was in the sixth grade. The person called out about four names, including mine.

We were told to leave for another room. I discovered that I was being placed into a "special class" for "special kids." Kids that perhaps weren't as bright or quick at learning math or reading as the others.

Rather than trying to figure out what was going on in my personal life, I was pigeonholed as a child that had a learning disability. This just created more anxiety and hopelessness within me.

Many times kids can be incredibly cruel and malicious in pointing out your challenges. I can recall the jeering and mocking that took place at recess when my friends found out that Danny was now in the "stupid class." Now I was not only different because my dad's death, but also because I was considered slower than the rest of the class.

Looking back, I can now see how the Lord had His hand in our family all along. Our father's relationship with his children was very strained, to say the least, and quite dysfunctional for the most part. The choice that he made to end his life forced me as a child to understand that I couldn't take anything for granted.

The very things that we many times assume would always be there can be completely taken in an instant. This experience forced me to look at life from a more eternal perspective. I could sense that I now saw the world differently than most children my age. Reality was glaring at me straight in the face, and life had now lost its innocence.

A few years after my father's untimely death, our mother began to attend a new church. The church that our family was involved with before his death became too difficult for my mother to attend due to the stigma of being a suicide's widow.

One Sunday evening when Mom was leaving for the evening service, I asked her where she was going. She said, "I'm trying out a new church. Do you want to come?" Surprisingly to her, I said yes, and off the two of us went to try out this new place of worship. She told me years later that when I agreed to go, she almost burst into tears of joy. Her prayer was being answered.

Once in the service, I instantly knew that this was something different. Unlike our previous churches, in this new environment there was a freedom that I had never experienced before. People were worshipping God, but not in a dead religious type of way. You could tell it was genuine. Deep down inside, I knew that this is what I needed for myself.

For the next year, I attended the church's youth group. But due to the trauma my family was going through, my life was filled with continual fear and incredible anxiety. The allure of my own demise through suicide was never far from my thoughts. I thought that it was only a matter of time until I would finally give up on living.

On a fall weekend, the church had what was called their annual "North Western Youth Weekend." It was a time when several church youth groups from the surrounding area would come and hang out at our church for a few days. We slept in the church, played sports, and listened to special speakers who spoke at our level.

I was working at a local Safeway grocery store at the time, so I couldn't attend the Friday evening service. For some reason, I knew that I needed to be there, so as soon as I finished my shift, I raced over to the church, only to get there when the speaker was finishing his message. At this point, I didn't care what the preacher spoke about. I just knew that I needed to get to that altar. I ran to the front of the sanctuary with the desperate attitude of "Either you take my life or I will!"

Suddenly, God began to do something within me that I had never felt before. The first thing was that I began to cry. This was a miracle in and of itself. Up to this point, I had not yet cried over my father's death. He had been dead for three years, yet still I refused to weep for him. I bottled it all up inside and never went through any proper mourning period.

Once I started to cry, I couldn't stop. I then began to raise my hands and press into God, pleading with Him to save my life. I didn't want to die, but I didn't want to live with this pain any longer. Once I began to raise my hands and cry out to God, I suddenly began to do something that for a 16 year-old non-Pentecostal boy, with his peers all around him, was neither cool nor appealing.

I began to speak in an unknown language. I had no idea what I was doing; all I knew was that God was doing something amazing inside my spirit. Later on the pastor told me that I was speaking in tongues and was filled with the Holy Spirit. As a 16 year-old young man, this really didn't make much sense to me, but I didn't care. I felt alive. For the first time in years, I felt peace in my heart.

Moments after being filled with the Holy Spirit, I remember the pastor encouraging us to be quiet before the Lord because He was about to say something to us. As I sat there listening intently to the Holy Spirit, I heard Him whisper to my heart, "Danny, I'm going to use you in ministry."

"Ministry? What in the world is ministry?" I thought to myself.

I didn't know what this meant, and I definitely didn't think that He meant being a pastor. Because of the abuse that my father put us through, I became a very introverted child. I never wanted to stand out in a crowd, and even when I spoke, many times I would stammer in my speech. Therefore, the thought of being called to ministry would have to be anything but public speaking.

The weekend ended and each of us went back to our everyday lives, but something definitely changed within me. I still had a long way to go, but deep down inside I knew that God was placing me on a different path than I was expecting. The seed was germinating.

Within a few years of that experience, I began to drift away from this calling. I had graduated from high school and I now had a job at the same factory that my father worked at before he died. I was in an odd place emotionally. I was doing my very best to rebel, yet I wasn't very good at it! I was making incredible money for a 19 year-old and wasting a lot of it on stupid things and silly friends. The crazy thing was that I was also putting aside each payday a few hundred dollars, just in case I decided I wanted to go to Bible school.

Finally, one evening in a moment of despair, while in an environment that I knew better than to be in, the Lord clearly said, "Go home, apply for Bible school and get going! I have work for you to do!"

And with that, in September of 1987, at the age of 20, I found myself in Bible school. I was absolutely terrified, but smack dab in the middle of God's will.

What brought me to that place? What brought me to that moment in my life where I was now considering clerical ministry? It was the deep, desperate valleys in my childhood that forced me to listen to that still small voice of God's Holy Spirit.

I truly believe that if it had not been for those traumatic experiences, I probably would not have been prepared or even interested in going down this path. The exposure to pain has the power to do that.

John McDonnell says that, "Every problem introduces a person to himself. Each time we encounter a painful experience, we get to know ourselves a little better. Pain can stop us dead in our tracks. Or it can cause us to make decisions we would like to put off, deal with issues we would rather not face, and make changes that make us feel uncomfortable."

As a dad, I am so proud of my kids. All three of them are growing up to be amazing young adults. My son, Jordan, for example, has an incredible passion and love for others. On Christmas Eve, 2016, around 10:30 in the evening, he went to the store with his sisters. After being gone for over an hour, I began to get a bit agitated. After all, family needs to be together on the night before Christmas morning.

At that point, my wife called our daughter on her cell phone to see where they were. Our daughter, Taylor, answered the phone and explained that Jordan was at the ATM machines talking to a homeless man and giving him some supper. Suddenly my frustration turned to absolute pride. I mean who does that? Especially on Christmas Eve?

That's just like Jordan. He has this passion in his life that has always been there. When he was just a little guy, I came into his room one evening and I could tell he was not his joyful self. I asked what was wrong. After a little prodding, he answered me, "How come my sisters don't have the same problems that I have? How come I'm the one with the braces, the glasses, the asthma, a hearing problem (an issue that he has since been miraculously healed from), and my sisters have none of those things?"

Quickly the Lord showed me what to say. "Jordan," I responded, "When God has His calling on our lives, He has to allow difficulties to happen to us. It is only trials that help us understand and sympathize with the sufferings in our cruel world."

I could see in his eyes that he understood what I meant, and it seemed to lighten his dampened spirit. All these years later, that passion for others has never left Jordan's heart. His heart is huge and it took his painful experiences to get him there.

CHAPTER 3

SQUARE PEGS IN ROUND HOLES

As followers of Christ, Jesus warned us that we would be looked upon as being different from the world. In 1 Peter 2:11 (NASB), we are told, "Beloved, I urge you as aliens and strangers to abstain from fleshly lusts which wage war against the soul."

When you think of someone who is an alien or stranger, you can quickly visualize a creature from another planet, or someone who lives in a completely different part of the world. And although I don't believe that Peter had little green men in mind when comparing us to aliens, he was trying to stress that we are in this world but definitely not of it. Once we surrender our lives to Christ, as believers we quickly find ourselves dwelling in unfamiliar surroundings.

Whenever I travel to another part of the world, I am quickly overcome with the sense that I am out of my comfort zone. Everything from the food, the language and the customs are completely foreign to me.

I remember a time back in 2007 when I was involved in doing some outreach crusade services in the countries of Burundi and Uganda. This was my first time in Africa and I clearly remember how everything was so strange to me.

After being there for almost two weeks, eating local food and trying to adapt to the culture the best we could, one afternoon my colleagues and I stumbled across a local pizzeria in downtown Kampala, Uganda. I remember the look on our faces when we were finally able to eat food that we were familiar with. To us, it was the most incredible pizza that we had ever had. In hindsight, it probably wasn't all that amazing, but at that moment, it was a little taste of home.

When it comes to the believer, Jesus warns us that this is the same reality when we put our faith in Christ. Once we are in Christ, 2 Corinthians 5:17 tells us, "The new creation has come, the old has gone, the new is here!" Upon committing your life to Christ, you will never feel at home in your old ways ever again.

No longer will you feel a part of this world, any more than a fish does on dry land. It is almost as if your DNA had actually changed the moment of your salvation. Even before you came to know the Lord, you were unknowingly on a spiritual collision course with the Holy Spirit.

You didn't realize it, but the Lord knew that the day was coming when you would finally come to your senses and understand what you were created to do, to bear much fruit for the Lord. In other words, you were an alien before you knew you were an alien.

You were like the cat, in a video I once saw, who was raised by rabbits. In the video, the cat learned to jump around like a rabbit because that was what its adopted mother taught him. His DNA said otherwise. But in his little mind, he was a rabbit and nobody could tell him otherwise.

Many of us, before we came to the Lord, thought that we were just like everyone else. We talked like them, we behaved like them, and yes, we even sinned like them. However, deep within our heart, we sensed that there was something different about us. The truth is that you were created to bear much fruit for God's Kingdom.

You felt like that old adage of being a square peg in a round hole. You couldn't explain it, but you knew that you were being called up to something better. May I add that there is nothing more miserable than someone who is fighting the Holy Spirit and trying to live like everyone else.

They are the cat who is determined to live their life as a rabbit, but they know something is just not right. I'm sure if that cat at some point saw himself with his siblings in a mirror, he would have thought, "Hey something's not adding up!"

The rebellious believer is no different. If they were honest with themselves, they would know that something was just not adding up. They would know that it was time to come to grips with who they were created to be.

UNEASY FEELING

With this perspective in mind, I want to take this concept a bit further. Just as the child of God is very much an alien in the world, within the community of born-again believers, there are also individuals who feel different. Perhaps they even feel awkwardly out of place from their fellow brothers and sisters in Christ.

Many would call it restlessness within their spirit that keeps convicting them that they are called to something higher.

Understand that a calling is what God gives to individuals, not as something that is better, but something that is different. Because it is a part of your spiritual DNA, the calling is a restless burden that the individual cannot ignore. It is this "something different" that the called will at times beg the Lord to remove from their lives.

Jeremiah understood this inner battle very well when he wrote in Jeremiah Chapter 20:7b-9:

"I am ridiculed all day long; everyone mocks me. Whenever I speak,

I cry out proclaiming violence and destruction. So the word of the Lord has brought me insult and reproach all day long. But if I say, "I will not mention his word or speak anymore in his name," his word is in my heart like a fire, a fire shut up in my bones. I am weary of holding it in; indeed, I cannot."

Trying all you might to keep that calling bottled up will only bring misery and despair in the life of the called. When one chooses to walk in the path of the called, you will find yourself on a sometimes lonely, isolated road that those who do not have the calling cannot understand nor relate to its demands. Yet, until the called individual finally submits to the Lord's will for their life and stops resisting, like the backslidden believer, they'll remain in a state of misery.

UNHAPPY SOULS

For as long as the church has existed, there has been a group of people that we'll call the "unhappy souls." They attend churches, call themselves believers, and even involve themselves in church activities. Yet, when you study their lives, you will discover that their behavior shows that they fall into one of these two categories:

A. THE UNCOMMITTED

The first category are those we will call the "uncommitted." These are the people who have never really devoted themselves to the Lord in the first place. They are the ones who drank the Kool-Aid of seeker-sensitive Christianity. They avoid the Matthew 16:24 challenge where Jesus says, "Whoever wants to be my disciple must deny themselves and take up their cross and follow me."

They believe that a full denial of self is unnecessary for a blessed filled life since Jesus paid it all, therefore they don't have to.

Also within this group of the uncommitted are those who have been taught and understand the full council of God. They do understand the challenge of committing one's everything to the Lord, they just don't want to. Like the rich young ruler, they refuse to do so because the cost seems too high. They claim that the Lord is everything, yet by their actions, their lives tell a different story.

The second group of unhappy souls are:

B. THE CHOSEN

These individuals consist of those who have a special calling on their lives. They are frustrated because, despite having a calling, they have bought into the lie that if they just behave like every other normal believer that they know, and ignore their God given destiny, that their life would be at peace. Because of their disobedience and unwillingness to step out and listen to the calling that God has placed on their lives, they remain unfulfilled and live with the "Is this all there is?" perspective of their Christian faith.

Personally, I have to admit that for a period of time I found myself living in this façade of being dishonest with myself.

As I mentioned earlier in my testimony, the Lord did an amazing thing in literally saving my life at the age of 16. During those years, I began to commit myself to the church and to its teachings. I began to hang around with other believers of my age. Although none of us were at all close to perfection, most of us did our best to encourage each other in our faith.

Yet even amongst my fellow Christian friends, I couldn't help but still feel that sense of being called to something different. Where many of my Christian peers were very comfortable in pursuing regular secular careers and paths in life, deep inside, the Holy Spirit kept pushing me to not be satisfied with the status quo.

Soon after being hired at the factory, the company took on an additional 100 new employees and my seniority very quickly shot through the roof. People would look at me and say, "How did a kid like you get such a good job in here?" I was making incredible money, but it didn't matter because deep in my heart, I knew I was called to something different.

Rather than saving money for a nice car, I began to save money for Bible school. And when I quit that job after just 1 1/2 years, even many of my Christian peers thought I was nuts for giving up such an opportunity!

I wasn't thinking I was any better than my peers, and, in fact, for the most part of those early years, I always felt a bit inferior to those around me. I couldn't understand why they didn't have that same burden that I did. Because of my insecurities in my youth, I chalked my feelings up to being just odd or different.

Those who God calls to a different form of work, whether that is church leadership, evangelism, missions, humanitarian work or whatever, according to Scripture, will almost always feel completely unqualified and ill prepared for the task at hand.

Ironically, those in Scripture who the Lord used and who did feel qualified, and who felt that God was lucky to have them on His side, be it Saul (later to become Paul), Peter, Samson or Jacob, were quickly put through the perils of life. Over time, this reminded them just how helpless they were without the Lord.

Although there are countless other heroes from the Scriptures that I could have used to bring home this point (whether Jacob, Daniel, Ruth, Gideon, Samuel, Jeremiah, and many, many more), for space and time, I've chosen to focus on three patriarchs of the Older Testament who had callings on their lives. Joseph, Moses and David, who although individually called, came from very different backgrounds and experiences.

Through the lives of these three men, we will find that when called by God, although it is a great privilege and honor, it will require great sacrifice, determination and commitment to actually fulfill the divine calling in ones life.

CHAPTER 4

DISTINCT CALLINGS IN CRUCIAL TIMES

If you are called, it's because God chose you to be used this way and not necessarily because you had all the natural abilities to lead. God knew that you would be one who would take all the challenges that have been placed before you and use them in making you more spiritually focused and mature!

Every one of us has had to deal with hurt and anguish in our lives in one form or another. When it comes to the patriarchs like Joseph, Moses and David, it wasn't any different. Joseph had his prisons, Moses had his deserts, and David had his caves! What set them apart as leaders and heroes of the Bible is how they dealt with their challenges.

You can take two people, especially siblings, who have gone through very similar trials in life and find that one has grown better and stronger through their challenges while the other chose to live as a victim, becoming weakened and bitter by these same tribulations.

When I consider my own testimony, I can clearly look back upon each and every trial as a tool that God was allowing me to experience in order to begin the preparation for the future work that the Lord prepared for me.

And by the way, those tests and trials will never end. The battles will continue throughout your life. Most times, they will grow even more invasive and difficult. However, each trial that we become victorious over, will prepare us for an even larger challenge down the road.

In other words, you will never handle grade one until you overcome the challenges of kindergarten. Your spiritual maturity is God's goal for you. Until you learn to grin and bear each challenge, each test as they come along, you will always remain spiritually immature in your own personal kindergarten class.

The writer of Hebrews says in Chapter 5:12b-14, "You need milk, not solid food! Anyone who lives on milk, being still an infant, is not acquainted with the teaching about righteousness. But solid food is for the mature, who by constant use have trained themselves to distinguish good from evil."

He also says earlier in verse 12a, "In fact, though by this time you ought to be teachers, you need someone to teach you the elementary truths of God's word all over again." Hmm, sounds like kindergarten to me.

The devil and his legion of demons know exactly how God is preparing to use you in unique ways to advance His Kingdom. The devil knows that God wants to develop you to teach and disciple others.

Therefore, the longer that he can keep you spiritually immature by keeping you on the milk bottle, the less threat he knows you will become against the kingdom of darkness. He will deploy all the weapons that are at his disposal in order to destroy your spiritual potential before it even has a chance to start.

The sad truth is, that throughout history, there have been countless men and women that God wanted to use in a powerful way for His Kingdom, people who had a calling. But because of the spiritual warfare and temptations that came with that calling, many surrendered to the devil before the victory was theirs. For some, like my father, whom I believe also had a calling on his life, they surrendered to the fullest extent by allowing the enemy to destroy their life all together. Which, of course, is the devil's ultimate plan for all of us (John 10:10).

For others, their surrender to the enemy is subtler. Their defeat lies in the sad reality of them not following God's calling at all. And if they did choose to serve the Lord to some degree, their immaturity made sure that they didn't create too many waves that may have caused them any discomfort or social awkwardness.

As mentioned earlier, they end up as unhappy souls, living unfulfilled lives, angry with God, and feeling that He somehow brought upon their trials as some kind of cruel joke. They never came to realize that perhaps each of these experiences were all a part of God's ultimate plan to prepare them for an amazing calling.

As we look at the patriarchs of Joseph, Moses and David, you will quickly discover that all of them had to go through basically the same spiritual training camps in order for God to achieve His goal for their lives. The only way that they were able to accomplish God's ultimate plan was to understand that there was a bigger picture for what God was allowing them to go through.

As Joseph proclaimed to his brothers at the end of his story, "You intended to harm me, but God intended it for good to accomplish what is now being done, the saving of many lives" (Genesis 50:20).

Regardless of the diversity and uniqueness of these men's experiences, each of them had their own distinct stories where their lineages, their lessons, and their legacies would be used by God to bring about His will for His people, Israel and the world.

In discussing their lineages, we will see a number of characteristics that these men of God had that every called individual also needs to possess in order to fulfill all that God has for them. These characteristics are stubbornness, proactiveness, determination, individuality, compassion, humility, and self-reliance.

Just like all of us, these men displayed attributes and character qualities and flaws that were very much a part of their family's DNA. Looking at Joseph, the comparison to his family is very easily picked up since the Bible gives a very vivid storyline of Joseph's father, grandfather and great-grandfather.

In regard to Moses not so much. We really don't know anything about his father, Amran. We learn a bit about his loving mother, Jocobed and we read that it was his sister, Mariam, who watched him from the shore as his basket floated towards his destiny.

It is only Moses' brother, Aaron, that the Bible spends some time on, but even with him, the Bible is fairly limited as to who he really was as a person. We know that he was Moses' spokesman or prophet to Pharaoh during the exile and we know that he became the first of many High Priests of his family line in this new nation of Israel. This was a position he held until his premature death on Mount Hor for allowing Moses to strike the rock in the desert of Zin.

Regarding David, we will discover his lineage has some fairly impressive connections to biblical heroes, such as Baoz and Ruth. But, regarding his father, Jesse, and his brothers, the Bible is somewhat quiet on the topic and leaves much to the imagination.

Despite what we don't know, what we DO know, as we will discover, says a lot about who these men became and why the Lord called them in the first place.

CHAPTER 5

THE CALLING OF JOSEPH

LINEAGE OF JOSEPH

There is a quote that says, "Every son quotes his father, in words and in deeds," which I would say is a very good description of Joseph's lineage. Joseph's father, Jacob, was known as someone who some would call a bit of a character. Despite being a mama's boy, Jacob was able to swindle his older brother, Esau, out of his birthright over a measly bowl of soup.

Even when Isaac, his father, was about to die, Jacob's mother, Rebecca, convinced him to wrap animal hair on his arms to convince his blind father that he was his hairier older brother, Esau, in order to receive the first-born's blessing. Well, it worked.

For years after, Jacob was always looking over his shoulder, fearing the backlash of a vengeful brother who lost his birthright to his deceptive younger brother. What kind of person does that kind of thing? I'm guessing it's the same kind of person that we later find in Genesis 32 physically wrestling with God!

Jacob had a mischievous character that God had to deal with in order to take him to the next level in his walk with the Lord. God had blessed him, yet, God had to deal with his attitude. We have all heard of the saying, "What goes around comes around," and that's exactly what happened to Jacob.

After stealing Esau's blessing from his father at his mother's request, Jacob flees to his Uncle Laban's house. While there, Jacob falls in love with Laban's younger daughter, Rachel. Rather than taking wages for his services for working for his uncle, he asks that Rachel would be given to him as his wife if he worked for Laban for seven years.

Laban agrees, and after seven years of work, we read in Genesis 29:21-27:

"Then Jacob said to Laban, "Give me my wife. My time is completed, and I want to make love to her." So Laban brought together all the people of the place and gave a feast. But when evening came, he took his daughter Leah and brought her to Jacob, and Jacob made love to her. And Laban gave his servant Zilpah to his daughter as her attendant. When morning came, there was Leah! So Jacob said to Laban, "What is this you have done to me? I served you for Rachel, didn't I? Why have you deceived me?" Laban replied, "It is not our custom here to give the younger daughter in marriage before the older one. Finish this daughter's bridal week; then we will give you the younger one also, in return for another seven years of work."

I would love to have been a fly on the wall the next morning when Jacob woke up the day after his wedding only to see Leah lying there beside him! The deceiver became the deceived! Is it possible that God had something to do with this? Of course, He did. What went around came around. How interesting that in verse 25b he asks his father-in-law, "Why have you deceived me?"

When the Lord is preparing us for the calling, He has an amazing way of giving us a taste of our own bad medicine. Without it, we would never understand the pain that our misbehavior has caused others. In order to obtain the most valuable attribute of a spiritual leadership, which is servanthood, one has to learn to serve.

And for 14 years, Jacob did just that. He served his father-in-law in order to obtain the right to marry Rachel. In those 14 years, Jacob's heart began to change.

His heart changed so much that the day came when Jacob realized it was time to make amends with his brother, Esau. He chose to return to Canaan. He knew that if God was going to bless him, as he had prayed in Genesis 32:9-12, God would require him to once and for all face the music of his assumed vengeful brother.

As mentioned in my testimony, during my childhood, my father's behavior caused our family incredible pain and anxiety. I mentioned how at the age of 16, after my father's death, God began to touch my life and prepare me for the ministry that lay before me. Yet, I have to admit, as we all do, that healing doesn't happen overnight and many times forgiveness takes a while to achieve.

In 1991, after four years of study, I was about to graduate from Bible school. During the last weeks of school, we had special services that were called, "Spiritual Emphasis Days." During these services, God began to show me how I still hadn't completely forgiven my father for what he did to our family.

In fact, I can clearly remember the Lord saying to me, "You will never be able to minister to others until you allow me to minister to you." With that revelation, the Lord forced me to see my father through God's eyes.

I began to receive visions of my dad as a child in Germany during the war, the stories that I heard about but never paid much attention to. I had visions of when he was starving and terribly malnourished, which affected his health right up to his death. I could see in my mind images of both my father and his brother standing in the barn and looking up at their father, hanging from a rope after taking his own life.

God began to ask me, "When are you going to learn to let him go? Just like you, he was broken, yet now you have the opportunity to do something with your pain. Give it to me and you will never look back."

It was because of this revelation of my dad that suddenly I began to convulse with tears. I lay at the altar and wept for what seemed like hours.

But, this time I was no longer weeping over my own pain, but now weeping over what my father kept bottled up for so many years. I felt nothing but pity for him. I wanted to reach out into eternity and tell my dad that I forgave him, that I understood more clearly why he did what he did.

These revelations didn't justify and make right what he did. But it certainly forced me to reflect on who he was and why he behaved like he did. I was being healed and my healing was preparing me for another step closer to the calling God had for me.

In the story of Jacob in Genesis 32:6, while he is on his way back to the land of Canaan, he gets word that his brother is coming to meet him with 400 men. Jacob, assuming the worst, separates his family and sends ahead gifts to meet Esau's army in hopes that it might appease his anger. However, as we find out in Chapter 33, this turned out to be unnecessary, because the Lord had dealt with the heart of Esau as well.

Just as I was able to see my father from God's point of view and receive healing for my future, God also did a miracle in both the hearts of Jacob and Esau so that they were both able to see each other through God's eyes.

James 4:6 tells us that, "God opposes the proud but gives grace to the humble." And the one thing that God was working on in Jacob's life while he worked for his father-in-law for these 14 years was his pride.

You can never truly serve in the capacity that the Lord desires until your pride is broken. We see in Genesis 32:22-32 that this character flaw of Jacob's is finally confronted once and for all. While waiting to hear how his estranged brother responds to the gifts that he sent on ahead, it is here, in a place that Jacob would call Peniel, that we read about Jacob's wrestling match with God.

What is this moment all about? What was God trying to show Jacob in allowing him this physical confrontation? Was it to convince Jacob just how tough he was, that he was one with the gods? I mean seriously, how many guys have bragging rights about something like that? Or was it actually to show the exact opposite? To show how weak in himself that Jacob really was? The answer can quickly be found in the following verses.

After wrestling with the angel of the Lord all night, we read in verses 25-28, "Then the man said, "Let me go, for it is daybreak." But Jacob replied, "I will not let you go unless you bless me." The man asked him, "What is your name?" "Jacob," he answered. Then the man said, "Your name will no longer be Jacob, but Israel, because you have struggled with God and with humans and have overcome."

From what I understand from verse 24, Jacob had initially no idea who he was wresting with. In fact, we know this by verse 30, "So Jacob called the place Peniel, saying, "It is because I saw God face to face, and yet my life was spared." It was only after that encounter that Jacob came to the stunning realization, "Um, that was God I wrestled with... and He allowed me to live!"

When it comes to our trials and moments of wrestling with the Lord, most of us have no idea how supernatural that moment was until after the fact. There are times when in the process of God developing that servant attitude in a called individual's life that God will allow some incredible moments of pain, of wrestling, in order to break our stubborn streak like an unbridled mule.

The times I have spoken with my peers who had just endured some very difficult moment in their personal life or ministry, they would many times describe the experience almost as if it had been a physical confrontation or battle.

I would say that Jacob's "wrestling with God" moment was a very unique, rare occasion. During our own attacks of the enemy, who is determined to destroy our ministry, God will use those struggles to chip and mold our character. He will continue breaking our pride and ultimately forming us into the image of Christ himself.

Think about this for a moment. God allowed a man like Jacob to physically wrestle with Him. Here's a guy who had a physical altercation with the angel of God all night and when the angel of the Lord tells him to let him go, Jacob replies by saying, "I will not let you go unless you bless me." Jacob's personality was such that he would pretty well do anything to get ahead and survive, even something like wrestling with someone whom he knew was from the Lord.

And it is here that we are introduced to the first characteristic that is many times contributed to a called person.

STUBBORNNESS

One might never think that a seemingly negative personality trait like stubbornness would actually be an asset to someone who is called. Yet when you look at an individual like Joseph's father, Jacob, you begin to realize that this seemingly negative character flaw was definitely an asset of Jacob's that God was going to use. It was only the terrible pride thing that went along with his stubbornness that God had to wrestle into submission.

There are many people in leadership today who are natural leaders, the Type A kind of people. In a dog-eat-dog world, they would be the ones who would even wrestle with God to accomplish their dreams. Sadly, many of these same Type A personalities spend their whole lives unknowingly wrestling with God rather than acknowledging Him. Many times they become successful in business and leadership; however, many of them fall far short in acknowledging where this gift comes from.

They are a personality that can very easily give in to the sin of pride and arrogance, believing that their accomplishments are a direct result of something they personally had done. Therefore, when these types of people have their moment of revelation with the Lord, they, like Jacob, are usually left living the rest of their lives with a limp, or, in the Apostle Paul's case, a "thorn in his flesh." It is a reminder of where their blessings come from. (See 2 Corinthians 12:7-9.)

During the time of Jacob's grandfather, Abraham, God was about to intervene in human history and begin the process towards bringing salvation to the world through the coming Messiah, Jesus. Because of this, He would first begin with a people, a nation who did not yet exist. So, whom did He begin with? He began with a man named Abram, later to be called Abraham, who we quickly find out from his character was a man with great determination.

I believe a big part as to why God chose Abraham was because of his spiritual DNA, which we find out included stubbornness. We are told in Genesis 12:1-4a, "The Lord had said to Abram, "Go from your country, your people and your father's household to the land I will show you. I will make you into a great nation, and I will bless you; I will make your name great, and you will be a blessing. I will bless those who bless you, and whoever curses you I will curse; and the peoples on earth will be blessed through you." So Abram left, as the Lord had told him."

Abram had no idea where God was taking him. Yet, when he heard from the Lord that it was time to leave his family, he went! It is here that we witness the second attribute that is essential in the life of someone who is called by God.

PROACTIVENESS

When it came to Joseph's lineage, you quickly discover, especially in Abraham, that these were a proactive, let's get it done, type of people. I believe that God has a special place in His heart for leaders like this.

When God told Abraham to leave home and go where God would lead him, he immediately left the only life and people he ever knew. When God told him that he would be the father of many nations, Abraham, although an older man, thought, "Okay, I don't know how You're going to do this, but let's get it done."

When both he and his wife, Sarah, felt that God was taking too long in providing them a son, his let's get it done attitude caused him to take matters into his own hands, and as we know, Ishmael was born through Sarah's maidservant, Hagar. His impatience in God's timing caused Abraham to try to help God along.

To this very day, because of God's promise to bless all of Abraham's descendants, the nations that were derived from Ishmael have been at odds with the descendants of Jacob ever since.

Despite Abraham's shortcomings, God blessed Abraham and Sarah with the miracle child, Isaac. When God asked Abraham to sacrifice this miracle child, once again, Abraham's faith shone through and with his let's get it done attitude, the Bible says, "Early the next morning Abraham got up and loaded his donkey" (Genesis 22:3).

That same determination, that can so easily cause the called individual to be sidetracked and taken down the proverbial rabbit trail of wrong choices, when directed by the Holy Spirit, can be proactive and can accomplish amazing things to change the world.

According to Scripture, Jesus has a strong disdain for incomplete tasks. Jesus said in John 15:11 (emphasis added), "I have told you this so that my joy may be in you and that your joy may be COMPLETE."

Did you catch that last word? Jesus wants our joy to be complete, finished, brought to its greatest potential. Whatever calling He has placed upon you, completing it is His ultimate goal.

The reason why so many believers' joy isn't complete is that what the Lord has ordained for their lives has not been allowed to be completed! And why is that? Because, they were not proactive in completing the task. They fell short of their divine calling.

In Luke 14:28-30 (emphasis added), Jesus says, "Suppose one of you wants to build a tower. Won't you first sit down and estimate the cost to see if you have enough money to COMPLETE it? For if you lay the foundation and are not able to finish it, everyone who sees it will ridicule you, saying, 'This person began to build and wasn't able to finish.'"

In a sense, we also see this mindset revealed in the church of Laodicea in Revelations 3:15. Jesus tells them, "I know your deeds, that you are neither cold nor hot. I wish you were either one or the other! So, because you are lukewarm—neither hot nor cold—I am about to spit you out of my mouth."

In other words, you are either all in or you are all out. Make up your mind!

If you are only lukewarm, you are not committed, and you will be tempted to quit the first time that you are confronted with the smallest of spiritual opposition. The success of the called individuals is very much based upon their proactive and determined attitude.

Joseph's lineage was from the 'all in' kind of stock. The plan for the nation of Israel would have never made it past the first or second generation if they just gave up the moment problems came their way.

The problem with many called believers is that their lives haven't reached their greatest potential. They haven't reached their completeness, because they don't aim to finish the task.

Many years ago, my stepfather gave me the book, The Prayer of Jabez, written by Bruce Wilkerson. I totally devoured that little book and have been praying that prayer for my family and myself for many years. I have also preached on this passage several times as well. In that book, he mentions a story about Mr. Jones.

Mr. Jones dies and goes to heaven. When he arrives, St. Peter is waiting at the Pearly Gates and takes Mr. Jones on a tour of heaven. Mr. Jones is awestruck. The streets are paved with gold, beautiful mansions glisten in the sunshine, choirs of angels sing the most beautiful songs. Partway through his tour of heaven, Mr. Jones' eye is drawn to an odd-looking building, an enormous warehouse with no windows and just one door. What an odd structure for heaven!

"You don't really want to see what's in there," says St. Peter.

"But I do, I do," says Mr. Jones.

He races across the lawn and pushes open the door to discover rows and rows of shelves, floor to ceiling. Stacked on the shelves are thousands of white boxes. The boxes all have names on them.

"Is there one with my name on it?" asks Mr. Jones as he rushes to the J aisle. He finds the box with his name on it and opens it up. His mouth drops, his pulse quickens, and finally he says to St. Peter, "What are all these wonderful things inside my box? Are they the good things in store for me now I've reached heaven?"

"No," replies St. Peter. "They're all the blessings God wanted to give you while you were alive on earth, but which you never received."

A sad look came over Mr. Jones. He looked into the box, to St. Peter and then back to the box. "Why?" he asked St. Peter. "Why did I miss out on all these blessings?"

"Because you never asked," St. Peter replied.

You will never be able to reach the fullness of your calling until you learn to aim to complete the task.

DETERMINATION

The next characteristic of a called individual is determination. One might argue that this is one and the same as one who is proactive. But as we look closer, we can see it goes much deeper than just focusing on finishing what we started. Any parent who has had a "determined" child knows that if not brought under proper guidance and discipline, this characteristic can cause a fair bit of misery for everyone involved. Spiritually speaking, for the called man or woman who has a "determined" attitude, it is not any different. Until this trait is finally dealt with and brought under the submission and guidance of the Holy Spirit, it can cause a man or woman to veer completely off course from God's will for their lives and head straight for self-destruction.

A case in point was Jonah. His determination not to do God's will almost not only caused his own death, but also the death of every crew member on that ship headed for Tarshish. Yet when guided and put under the submission of God's will, with the help of a big fish, this same characteristic of determination helped save the entire City of Ninevah.

Despite what personality type you may have been labeled with, whether you consider yourself an extrovert or introvert, or somewhere in between, the one aspect of what keeps a called person going is that stubborn determination to keep pressing on despite what others around you are choosing to do.

Abraham had it, Jacob had it, and we can see by his character, that it was passed down to his son, Joseph, as well.

In my chapter on David, I will be talking about my spiritual father, Alon Barak, who came into my family's life over 13 years ago. Alon was a former Jewish messianic rabbi in California, who now lives in Israel with this lovely wife, Ronnit. I have been blessed to call him my spiritual "dad" and he has empowered my understanding of God's Word on so many levels. In fact, he is the main reason why I was able to co-write my first book, <u>The Beauty of Jesus Revealed in the Feasts</u>, and it is to him that I dedicated that book.

One time while we were fishing walleye in Northern Ontario, Canada, he asked me, "Do you know why God chose the Jews to bring forth Jesus the Messiah?" Without allowing me to answer, he then asked another question, "Was it because we were so good?" "Not at all," again, answering his own question. "It's because we were so bad and so stubborn! God was showing the world that if He could change them, He can change anyone."

Looking back now, I can see what he meant. I can also see how this rings true when tied in with the calling and the Older Testament patriarchs. When it came to Jacob and Abraham, the one attribute that God desired to use was their stubbornness. He had to take that character flaw, that many would have seen as a deterrent to any calling, and twist and mold it into something that would, in the end, become something that was actually necessary and essential for the survival of God's people, Israel.

Recently, Alon shared with me another story about a friend of his, Louis Kaplin. Alon takes the story from here:

"In 1976, I invited Mr. Kaplin to be a guest speaker at my church in Jersey, Ohio. In 1967, Kaplin began a radio ministry called "The Jewish Voice Broadcast." This ministry was based in Phoenix, Arizona and was a 15-minute daily program.

"On his visit to our church, I picked Louis up from his hotel and on the way to the church, he asked me a life-changing question. "What is faith?" he asked. Quickly, like any good pastor, I quoted Hebrews 11:1, "Faith is the substance of things hoped for, the evidence of things not seen." In response, Louis said nothing for what seemed like eternity. When he finally spoke, his answer came unexpectedly, out of nowhere, "NO," he said sternly, "Faith is STUBBORNESS!"

"For most of the remaining trip after that we had silence. I was speechless. I have never forgotten him, and I shall never forget his towering, huge definition of faith. I later learned that Louis and his definition is 100% correct, and in fact very Jewish. It goes all the way back to Father Abraham and his conversation with the Lord."

As I said with the attribute of the called being proactive, the same rings true for stubbornness and determination. The reason why Israel still exists today, after thousands of years, despite nations trying to destroy them over and over again, is because of this God anointed stubborn determination embedded in their spiritual DNA. God's protection has continued to be upon them for thousands of years, because His promise remains with them that they would never be destroyed. When your back is against the wall, and you have the whole world wanting to destroy you, it is only this Holy

Stubbornness that will keep you going and prevent you from giving up.

If you are one who is called into some form of ministry, let me tell you, sometimes it will only be your spiritual stubbornness that will keep you determined to keep doing what God has called you to do.

Joseph was the grandson of Abraham and the son of Jacob. The DNA that lived in them was very much alive and well in Joseph. It was the very reason why he was chosen, from out of his brothers to fulfill God's will for Israel.

LESSONS OF JOSEPH

I am sure that when Joseph woke up that fateful morning after being sold into slavery by his brothers, he had no idea that his entire life was about to change.

At his father's request, going out to check on his brothers while they were tending his father's sheep, you would think he would have received at least a little gesture of gratitude. But, the animosity that his older brothers had against young Joseph had been building for some time. We witness this in Genesis 37:3-7 where we read:

"Now Israel loved Joseph more than any of his other sons, because he had been born to him in his old age; and he made an ornate robe for him. When his brothers saw that their father loved him more than any of them, they hated him and could not speak a kind word to him. Joseph had a dream, and when he told it to his brothers, they hated him all the more. He said to them, "Listen to this dream I had: We were binding sheaves of grain out in the field when suddenly my sheaf rose and stood upright, while your sheaves gathered around mine and bowed down to it." His brothers said to him, "Do you intend to reign over us? Will you actually rule us?" And they hated him all the more because of his dream and what he had said."

For those of you who grew up with younger siblings, you might be forgiven for having a little sympathy towards Joseph's older brothers. There is no doubt that Joseph was treated a little more special than the rest of his siblings. It's interesting that in the story of David, it was David who was out with the sheep and his brothers were home. In this story, it was the opposite. Joseph is the one home, while his brothers are out doing the laborious work of taking care of the sheep.

Being the first-born son to their father's favorite wife, Rachel, Jacob never hid the fact that Joseph held a special place in his heart. He even garnished him with an expensive coat of many colors while his envious brothers looked on. And then there were those dreams! Oh, the dreams! Can you imagine being one of Joseph's brothers listening as this 17 year-old kid began to interpret the visions that God gave him? Dreams that showed one day his brothers would be bowing down to Joseph and paying him honor.

Yeah, I could see why they might have felt a bit annoyed at Joseph's company and why they may have wanted to see a little less of him around the house.

However, in his youthful innocence and immaturity, we see no evidence that Joseph knew in these early days exactly how his brothers felt about him. I'm sure when he shared the meaning of his dreams to his family he had no idea of the animosity that he was creating in his brothers' hearts toward him. He was just doing what many enthusiastic young people do, speak without thinking and act without considering the consequences.

There's a reason why they send young men off to war rather than those who are middle aged. It's because at that age, very few young people think of the consequences. They think about the valor and the potential heroism that awaits them. They have no clear understanding of what might happen if they are wounded or worse.

Young Joseph had a calling on his life; there is no denying that. It was real. By providing those dreams, the Lord was giving young Joseph just a glimpse of what awaited him. Yet it is here that we are confronted with the first lesson when it comes to the calling.

FOCUS ON THE GROWTH, NOT THE GOAL

John Maxwell says the following: "If you focus on goals, you may hit goals - but that doesn't guarantee growth. If you focus on growth, you will grow and always hit goals."

I love that quote because it tells me that really anyone can hit incredible goals in their lives, as long as they focus on the growth and endure the journey!

As young David was busy growing and maturing while alone shepherding his father's herds, Joseph's focus was on his future goals of leadership. Rather than taking the opportunity to learn what he needed to develop in those early years, his mind was transfixed on the grandeur of being a ruler. Little did he know about the valley of suffering he would have to endure before those dreams would become a reality.

If you are one who senses a calling on your life, and perhaps you had dreams and prophecies spoken to you to verify this, always remember to focus on GROWTH today, not the GOAL tomorrow.

Each of our lives are filled with chapters and tests. As mentioned in Chapter 4, when you are in school, until you learn to master the teachings of one grade, you will not be able to move on to the next one.

The reason why the Hebrew people were in the wilderness for 40 years was not because the journey took that long, but rather, because they refused to learn their lessons while on the journey. Because they kept on making the same mistakes over and over again, they were forced to take another round over and over again.

It is the same with our lives. If we find that we are going through the same challenges over and over again, maybe it is because we keep on failing the same test. Just like Israel, we are forced to take another round.

For example, there would have been no way that David would have been able to handle Goliath unless he first passed the tests of the bear and lion.

The problem with Joseph, and many individuals who have a calling, is that they are already talking about the Goliaths that they are going to kill (the goal), yet they haven't even conquered their bears and lions (the growth).

Maybe you feel God is calling you to be a missionary sometime down the road. If you haven't been able to be a missionary in your own school, workplace or circle of friends, what makes you think you will succeed with the big things?

Before Joseph was to ever become a ruler over his brothers, he first needed to learn to serve them. And from my point of view, this is where young Joseph failed. He was so focused on the goals that he failed to grow. If you choose to grow rather than just accomplishing your goals, it is quite possible that you will be able to avoid your own 'empty well' and 'prisons' on your way to reaching those goals.

On several occasions during Jesus' ministry, His followers tried to force Him to become king because of the miracles they saw Him do.

In John 6:14-15, we read an example of this, "After the people saw the sign Jesus performed, they began to say, "Surely this is the Prophet who is to come into the world." Jesus, knowing that they intended to come and make him king by force, withdrew again to a mountain by himself."

Jesus withdrew again to a mountain by Himself when the crowds tried to force Him to become king, because Jesus understood His time had not yet come.

It takes a wise man or woman to understand the right timing for their future dreams and callings.

The Bible says in Ecclesiastes 3:7 that there is, "a time to be silent and a time to speak." This can so clearly relate to one's calling. There will be that time when you will speak, when you will teach and train, mentor and preach, or whatever that goal that you feel called to. But, don't forget that time of silence, that time of growth, that time of learning that must always precede the calling that God has placed in your heart.

I remember the original 1984 movie "Karate Kid" when a young boy named Daniel wanted to learn the martial arts from Mr. Miyagi. He wanted to be a competitive martial arts fighter and prove to some guys at his school that he was as tough as they were. One evening while he is being kicked and beaten by these same guys, Mr. Miyagi intervenes and saves Daniel from any further harm. Realizing that this elderly gentleman knew his stuff when it came to karate, Daniel asks him if he could train him in the arts.

Reluctantly, Mr. Miyagi agrees to do so. So, what does he do? Mr. Miyagi gets him to paint his house and to wash and wax his car, over and over and over again in the same repetitive pattern. The famous line in the movie is, "Wax on, wax off, wax on, wax off." If you haven't seen it, I encourage you to watch it!

After becoming completely frustrated because he felt that he was just Mr. Miyagi's servant, Daniel suddenly realized that those very repetitive motions that Mr. Miyagi taught him were movements that were precisely how Daniel was to protect himself in the martial arts. He was growing towards his goal; he just didn't know that he was.

That was exactly what was happening to David out in the field, and that was exactly what Joseph was still to experience on the way to his God ordained calling.

The writer of Hebrews reminds us in Chapter 12:11, "No discipline seems pleasant at the time, but painful. Later on, however, it produces a harvest of righteousness and peace for those who have been trained by it."

Training is never pleasant. Those wax on, wax off experiences that seem so mundane, and sometimes even painful at the time, will produce a great outcome if we focus on the growth and not only on the goal.

We read in Genesis 37:23-28:

"So when Joseph came to his brothers, they stripped him of his robe—the ornate robe he was wearing— and they took him and threw him into the cistern. The cistern was empty; there was no water in it. As they sat down to eat their meal, they looked up and saw a caravan of Ishmaelites coming from Gilead. Their camels were loaded with spices, balm and myrrh, and they were on their way to Egypt. Judah said to his brothers, "What will we gain if we kill our brother and cover up his blood? Come, let's sell him to the Ishmaelites and not lay our hands on him; after all, he is our brother, our own flesh and blood. His brothers agreed. So when the Midianite merchants came by, his brothers pulled Joseph up out of the cistern and sold him for twenty shekels of silver to the Ishmaelites, who took him to Egypt."

Don't miss that last word. Egypt. God had much in store for Jacob's descendants, but they first had to all end up in the pagan land of Egypt. And how were they going to get there? Through the traumatic experience of Joseph being sold by his brothers.

This leads us to the second lesson that the called can learn through the story of Joseph.

STAY TRUE TO YOUR CONVICTIONS

Recently, I found some old love letters that I sent my wife while we were still dating in college. I didn't even know that she kept them, but there they were, all nicely tucked away in a little box in her closet all these years. I picked one out and began to read. It was written on December 21, 1989, a day after her 20th birthday, while we were apart for the Christmas break.

As I read through this letter, what stood out to me was not only the passion I had for Lenise, but also for the calling. I was so excited about our future together and I couldn't wait for our first opportunity to minister. I won't bore you with all the lovey, dovey stuff, but this is what I wrote in the last paragraph:

"There is no way that the Lord can use me if I don't allow Him to have complete control of my life, thoughts and actions. So many times I feel as if I can live two separate lives, one for myself and one for Him. God forgive my shallow mindedness. Lenise, God has something incredible in store for us. I can just feel it. Let's never forget what Jesus did for us. We must give Him all of our lives, even to death! I love you, Lenise, but I love Him more, much more! Wow, where did that come from?! Well, my Neicey, I'll talk to you soon. Say hi to your family from me, I'm praying for them all."

As I finished reading this 30 year-old letter, I began to think where our lives went from there. I'll share more about our ministry years later on, but I will say here that after graduating from seminary two years later in 1991, Lenise and I married. Then, in 1992, we were offered our first youth pastor position on the east coast.

I remember saying to Lenise on the ride home from the interview, "We are going to make this pastor so happy that he hired me as his assistant!" I was determined to make this man proud and couldn't help but remember the words of a pastor friend of the family who said to us soon after our wedding, "Whatever you do, support your senior pastor and protect him."

This was what we resolved to do. Yet the moment I began this position, I quickly discovered that this was not what I expected it to be.

I remember meeting with the former youth pastor who had that position before me. He seemed very nervous and emotionally strained. He said nothing bad about the pastor, but then again, he never said anything good either.

Without going into much detail, in less than a year, I was an emotional wreck. I discovered later on that I was the third youth pastor that he had in three years. The following two years after my time there, he hired two more. Five in five years.

I won't say anything else about that experience except the one moment during our weekly staff meeting when he said to me, "Dan, I want you to remember, there is only room for one pastor here. I'm the pastor and you're my employee."

I will never forget that statement, because it completely rattled what I thought I was there for. I knew he was the senior pastor, but surely I wasn't just his employee. I thought I had a calling. I thought I had been given the opportunity to pastor these young people, and now I was being told that wasn't who I was here.

At that moment, I began to question everything I knew about being called. Perhaps it was just some crazy idea in my mind to go into full-time ministry. Perhaps it was never a part of God's plan in the first place and only something that I conjured up in my own head.

One day as I was sitting in my office, after being in this church only eight months, I was about to pick up the phone and call the factory that I used to work at to see if they could hire me back. Maybe that was all I was cut out for. Maybe this whole ministry thing was all a misguided idea that was never meant for a simple-minded guy like me.

As I was about to pick up the phone to call them, I was startled when the phone rang right in front of me. On the other end of the line was a fellow pastor who I knew as being a good friend of my senior pastor. They spent a lot of time together, so I was a bit apprehensive as to what I was about to say after he asked the following question, "Dan, I hear that you are resigning, can I ask you why?" Without sharing any obvious details, I began to give him the typical "God is leading me elsewhere" clichés, which he didn't at all buy.

He said, "Dan, don't you dare leave ministry because of what you are going through. You have a calling on your life, and if you leave now, you would be walking away from God's will for you and your wife." He then said something that left me speechless, because he was the last person that I thought I'd hear this from. He said, "Your pastor has some issues that he needs to deal with. You are not the problem, so don't you dare take this personal."

I'm sure there was at least ten seconds of dead air on the phone after those words. I didn't expect it from this gentleman and it took great courage on his part to say this to me. After a few more words of encouragement, he finished off the conversation by saying a prayer for me and wished me well. I hung up the phone and was speechless all that afternoon.

A few days later, there was a knock on my office door and there stood the mother-in-law of my senior pastor. You could tell she felt a bit awkward to be there with me, but seemed very determined to share what she needed to say. She said, "Dan, I want to you to know something about my daughter." As she began to explain some of the issues her daughter had, it became very clear as to why it was so difficult for Lenise and I to minister in this environment.

Again, just like the previous conversation, she wished me well in my ministry and encouraged me not to give up because of what I had experienced over those previous eight months.

These two people, to this very day, have no idea how much their few words meant to me. I was about to throw in the towel when it came to ministry. I was about to run back to the life that I felt was the only one I was suited for. I was about to completely reject the calling that I was so confident I had, as expressed in that letter to Lenise a few years earlier. Yet just over a few days, the Lord used two very unexpected people to help keep my calling on track.

Within hours, Joseph went from living in the comfort of his father's household to now, not even knowing if he would survive the day.

The Bible says that once Joseph arrived in Egypt, he was sold off to Potiphar, who was an official and captain of Pharaoh's guard. In Genesis 39:2, it basically describes the whole aspect of Joseph's calling when it says, "The Lord was with Joseph so that he prospered, and he lived in the house of his Egyptian master."

Despite Joseph's shortcomings as a younger brother at home, the Lord was still with Joseph and his calling was secure. Once on his own and away from his family, Joseph was able to quickly take stock of his situation and learn the lessons he needed to learn in his new profession as a slave.

He didn't demand justice. He made no apparent appeals to the authorities for the injustice that he was experiencing. Rather, he settled down and did what he had to do to not only survive, but also to thrive in his present circumstance.

To those who are called, always stay true to your convictions and calling no matter what your circumstances look like. Like me at my first church, you will have moments when all you want to do is run. It's called your survival instinct, and unless you learn to overcome those urges, you will never experience your greatest victories!

Joseph could have sat in the corner of the house and just pouted and cried about what his mean brothers did to him. Yet, I believe something inside of him said, "No, there's a lesson to learn here and I'm going to make the best of it," and because of that, his new master took notice of him.

Regarding my calling, everything changed the moment that I chose to stay in ministry after almost going back to my old job. In 1992, while on a holiday in Michigan at my cousins' home, I received a call from a pastor friend of mine, Wayne Parks, in Winnipeg, Manitoba, Canada.

I had spoken to him a few months earlier while I was going through the difficult time in my first church. My mother had encouraged me to call him for some advice. Wayne Parks had been my pastor in Thunder Bay when I first felt my calling at the age of 16. His wisdom and kindness meant a lot to me as a young man. Calling him when I was struggling in my first church seemed to be a smart thing to do.

So here I was in Michigan, of all places, and the phone rings with Wayne on the other end of the line. Somehow he was able to track me down. He says to me, "Dan, my assistant just resigned and I was wondering if you would be willing to come work with me in Winnipeg?" Well, to make a long story short, after resigning from my first church, I spent seven glorious years with Wayne and his wife, Carol. Lenise and I developed a wonderful ministry in that church and it was while we were there that we had our three children, Taylor (1996), Jordan (1998) and Aliyah (2000).

If I had given up after my first church, I would have missed out on some of the most amazing years of my ministry. The lives we were able to impact during those years is something that we will always cherish. And through technology like Facebook, we are able to stay connected with many of those kids, who today have families of their own.

Regarding Joseph, the Bible says that, "When his master saw that the Lord was with him and that the Lord gave him success in everything he did, Joseph found favor in his eyes and became his attendant. Potiphar put him in charge of his household, and he entrusted to his care everything he owned" (Genesis 39:4-5).

Not bad for a slave boy. He did his best despite his present circumstances, and the Lord kept His end of the bargain by blessing him. Everything was going wonderfully, but God had bigger plans for this young man. Those plans would require young Joseph to go back to the school of hard knocks in order to open up his next chapter. He had to go down a bit before the Lord would raise him up even further in his calling. We see in Genesis 39:6b-12 what happens next to Joseph.

"Now Joseph was well-built and handsome, and after a while his master's wife took notice of Joseph and said, "Come to bed with me!" But he refused. "With me in charge," he told her, "my master does not concern himself with anything in the house; everything he owns he has entrusted to my care. No one is greater in this house than I am. My master has withheld nothing from me except you, because you are his wife. How then could I do such a wicked thing and sin against God?" And though she spoke to Joseph day after day, he refused to go to bed with her or even be with her. One day he went into the house to attend to his duties, and none of the household servants was inside. She caught him by his cloak and said, "Come to bed with me!" But he left his cloak in her hand and ran out of the house."

Staying true to your convictions and calling will force you to make some difficult decisions from time to time. As we just read, Joseph was a well-built, handsome young man, and because of this, Potiphar's wife tried to take advantage of him.

Like any young man of his age, he had the same temptations and desires, but this is where we see the true MAN of Joseph rising up. It was in this moment that Joseph proved that he was more than just the son born in Jacob's old age, but was a rising leader that had a preordained calling and purpose.

When our higher calling is solidified in our heart and soul, it helps govern the moral compass in our lives. We choose to do, or not to do, things based upon our higher calling, because we believe we are created for a higher purpose.

I was a student in seminary in the late 80's when it seemed all the evangelical big boys were having their moral failures. I can remember watching it on the news and wondering to myself, "If big stars like these guys can't stand for moral purity, what hope do I have?"

You don't have to be a young man Joseph's age to fall morally from your convictions. You can be the leader of a great ministry, and have a huge following, and still miss the mark. Where these men failed, and where many in ministry fall, and not just with fornication, but with other moral failings as well, is when they lose the anointing of their unique calling. When they forget, even for just a very short period of time, who they are and the special and unique position that God had called them to, one can easily stray away from their divine purpose.

When David was on the balcony of his palace and he saw Bathsheba bathing, for that one moment, David forgot who he was and whom he represented. For that one moment, David was, in his thoughts, just a man who saw just a woman who just happened to be the wife of one of his armies' commanders.

And because he refused to control his thoughts and actions, that moment led to the biggest mistakes of David's Kingdom.

Joseph knew who he was going to be, even as a child. And although in his immaturity, he did not know how to appropriately express his calling to his family, even so, his calling and anointing was real.

When he was confronted by Potiphar's wife, Joseph's response was not that of a typical teenager, because Joseph knew that he wasn't typical. His response was that of a man who had his destiny in mind and nothing would distract him from that, even if he had to run from the temptation.

If you have a calling, you will always be that square peg in the round hole. You are set apart for a very special purpose. Therefore, expect the attacks, expect the temptations, but always be ready to run, because you don't have the privilege to fail.

As spiritual leaders, we are only as strong as our moral integrity. When that is gone, your divine destiny is weakened before your very eyes. Although God can restore, something is always lost. Because of his failure, David suffered the consequences of his actions. Not only was he denied the privilege of building the temple of the Lord (an honor that was passed down to his son, Solomon), but he also had to endure the infant death of his first-born son with his wife, Bathsheba.

Always stay true to your convictions and your integrity will continue to protect you throughout the journey of your calling. As Proverbs 10:9 so clearly states, "Whoever walks in integrity walks securely, but whoever takes crooked paths will be found out."

Once Potiphar's wife realized that her advancements were rejected, she felt humiliated and was determined to return the favor on young Joseph. We read in Genesis 39:16-20:

"She kept his cloak beside her until his master came home. Then she told him this story: "That Hebrew slave you brought us came to me to make sport of me. But as soon as I screamed for help, he left his cloak beside me and ran out of the house." When his master heard the story his wife told him, saying, "This is how your slave treated me," he burned with anger. Joseph's master took him and put him in prison, the place where the king's prisoners were confined."

A called individual must always remember this: Just because you choose to be a person of integrity and morality, don't expect the world to return the favor. The anti-Christ spirit that roams this earth hates everything about you. Therefore, when you choose to express righteousness and dignity over corruption and perversion, when you choose a calling from God that is committed to share the message of salvation, don't expect your adversary to take this lying down.

When Joseph showed up in the pagan culture of Egypt, light exposed its darkness. In the spiritual realm, Satan's legion of demons began to grow restless, knowing that God's anointed one was in town.

When Joseph resisted the temptation of Potiphar's wife, he was actually resisting Satan himself. And when the battle was as extreme and intense as it was for Joseph at that moment, all he could and should have done was exactly what he did. RUN!

There's no time for reasoning, no moment for silent reflection and prayer. When your enemy is surrounding you like a swarm of angry bees, you do what you need to do to survive. You run. You run so you can live to fight another day.

I'm sure it was Joseph that Paul was referring to when he wrote in 2 Timothy 2:22, "Flee the evil desires of youth and pursue righteousness, faith, love and peace, along with those who call on the Lord out of a pure heart."

Joseph survived that moment with his integrity intact. Because of that, he grew more confident, more determined and more focused in fulfilling his destiny. He passed that test and now he was about to endure another one in prison. In Genesis 39:20b-23, we read:

"But while Joseph was there in the prison, the Lord was with him; he showed him kindness and granted him favor in the eyes of the prison warden. So the warden put Joseph in charge of all those held in the prison, and he was made responsible for all that was done there. The warden paid no attention to anything under Joseph's care, because the Lord was with Joseph and gave him success in whatever he did."

Did you catch those repeated statements? Those just like verse 39:2? We are reminded that no matter what circumstance Joseph found himself in, "The Lord was with him." No matter how unfair the Lord might have seemed for allowing Joseph to be unjustly accused of attempted rape, the Lord had bigger plans.

Satan was working overtime to destroy this young man's destiny because he saw that something was brewing. Yet God was able to take what was evil and use it as Joseph's next launching pad, if Joseph allowed this to happen. It was completely up to how he responded.

Understand that all of this could have fallen off the rails for Joseph if he suddenly had a change of attitude and grew frustrated.

Think about it. After Joseph did the right thing and ran away from Potiphar's wife, he could have expected a little reward from the Lord for his actions. He could have thought, "Man, God has got to bless me now, because I didn't give in to temptation." Instead of being rewarded for his righteous behavior, the Lord allowed him to be sent to a dungeon, a place where Joseph could have easily believed that this was the end and that he was going to die there.

In your calling, you will find that there will be many good things you will choose to do that no one else notices. There will be charitable work or Godly choices that you will commit to just because it's the right thing to do. You will make those choices, not so that people will praise you for it, but because you know it pleases the Lord.

You might even be thinking in the back of your head, "Man, God has got to be so happy with me today!" Then suddenly, maybe even instantaneously, you go from that euphoric feeling to a sudden and cruel attack that seemed to come out of nowhere, that nasty phone call, that attack on your integrity or leadership decision that comes against you, etc.

It's at those moments that it can be very tempting to think, "This isn't worth it. It's not worth doing the right thing! It's too hard being a person of integrity when all you want to do is punch that person in the nose!" Don't forget where those thoughts are coming from. It's from the very pit of hell itself. It's in those moments that you have one of two choices. You can become complacent, bitter and cynical to your calling, which is exactly what the devil is aiming for, or you can choose to do what Joseph did. Keep on doing the right thing!

Unlike sin, where the gratification may be instantaneous and the regrets long-term, never forget, blessings are usually the opposite. When we do the right thing, there may not be an instantaneous reward, not one that we can see anyway. But the long-term blessings are eternal.

Joseph was not looking for the short-term blessings. He knew his dreams he had as a child were going to come true, and if it required a little time in the dungeon along the way, then so be it!

The moment he was thrown into prison, Joseph remained the man of integrity that he was just hours earlier in Potiphar's home, because although his surroundings might have changed, his attitude and integrity stayed the same.

This brings us to the next lesson that Joseph learned.

HOLD ONTO GOD TIGHTLY AND PEOPLE LOOSELY

There is no doubt that when you do the right thing, there will be those who will take notice and show their appreciation for your integrity. We see this with Joseph and the prison warden. He saw that Joseph was a young man who he could trust, and so he placed him in charge of all the other prisoners.

In prison, the Bible says that Joseph met two individuals, the King's cupbearer and the King's baker. Without going through all the details of the story, we are told that both of these men had dreams that Joseph was able to interpret for them.

With the cupbearer, Joseph was able to encourage him that his dream meant that in three days he would be restored to his position working for the King. In regard to the baker, the interpretation was much more sobering. His dream meant that in three days his body would be impaled to a pole and the birds would eat his flesh. Rather gruesome to say the least, yet this was exactly what happened.

When the cupbearer was being released from prison, Joseph tells him, "But when all goes well with you, remember me and show me kindness; mention me to Pharaoh and get me out of this prison" (Genesis 40:14).

You think that this would have been the least that this cupbearer could have done for Joseph. Instead, we read in verse 23, "The chief cupbearer, however, did not remember Joseph; he forgot him." For two more years, Joseph remained in that prison cell.

Now, let me ask you, if you were in Joseph's shoes, how would this scenario make you feel? If you are at all human, there would be a part of you, even a small part if you are close to perfect, that would feel a bit ticked off that the cupbearer forgot all about you in prison!

When you are called, and you are using your God-given gifts to help others, don't always expect any favors in return. If you are using your gifts and are hoping that you might receive perhaps just a little accolades from others, be prepared to be let down.

As a certified teacher of the John Maxwell Team, in one of my classes, I ask my students, "What would you say is your greatest asset, and what is your greatest weakness?" In asking that question, I have discovered that many people's greatest strength is also their greatest weakness.

My greatest strength is that I see the best in people. I have been able to pour love into some people that others have long ago given up on. It's been a joy over the years to see some of these individuals' lives change when they are confronted with the life-altering message of Jesus and their life is set on a new path.

Yet I have discovered, my same love for people and willingness to see the best in them has, as you can imagine, come back to bite me many times as well. When I love people, I just expected them to return the favor. Surprise, surprise. It does not always turn out that way. My failed assumption, that if I see the best in them that they would behave their best towards me, has come to hurt me on a number of occasions throughout my ministry.

The lesson I have learned here is NOT don't trust anyone. Rather, it is to understand that people are sinners. Even the most well-intentioned individuals will, at some point, let you down. It is just a matter of time. So, don't be shocked if and when that happens.

We have all met people in ministry whose hearts have become hardened and calloused over the years. I'm sure they did not start out that way or they would never have gone into ministry in the first place. Many of these individuals started out with good intentions, wanting to help people more than anything else. Unfortunately, over the years of living amongst the unappreciated, their focus was lost and their passion and calling damaged, and a heart was hardened.

By being sold into slavery by his own brothers, Joseph learned early on in life to be careful who to trust. Now in prison, Joseph is once again placing his hope in a fellow prisoner who promised to give a good word for Joseph when he was restored to his position as the King's Cupbearer.

Days turned into weeks and weeks into months. Months turned into years and yet Joseph heard nothing. I am sure that he could have grown a bit frustrated and disillusioned for using his giftings to help others only to be forgotten himself. I mean, what purpose does a calling serve if it helps everyone except the one who is called?

It is at these times that one must learn to hold onto God tightly and to people loosely. Putting our faith in people, hoping that they will somehow bless us for all our hard work, will inevitably lead to confusion and frustration.

If Joseph had allowed these feelings to overcome him, that would have ended the journey of his calling. He would have rotted in that prison cell, never to be heard of again.

Two whole years after the cupbearer was released from prison, Pharaoh has disturbing dreams that he could not interpret. He mentions them to his cupbearer and suddenly the lights come on and the cupbearer remembers his broken promise to Joseph.

"Then the chief cupbearer said to Pharaoh, "Today I am reminded of my shortcomings. Pharaoh was once angry with his servants, and he imprisoned me and the chief baker in the house of the captain of the guard. Each of us had a dream the same night, and each dream had a meaning of its own. Now a young Hebrew was there with us, a servant of the captain of the guard. We told him our dreams, and he interpreted them for us, giving each man the interpretation of his dream. And things turned out exactly as he interpreted them to us: I was restored to my position, and the other man was impaled." So Pharaoh sent for Joseph, and he was quickly brought from the dungeon. When he had shaved and changed his clothes, he came before Pharaoh. Pharaoh said to Joseph, "I had a dream, and no one can interpret it. But I have heard it said of you that when you hear a dream you can interpret it" (Genesis 41:9-15).

I love that last statement by Pharaoh to Joseph, "I have heard it said of you...." May I encourage you today, when you hold onto God tightly and people loosely, God will always reward you in the end for your integrity. Your reputation will precede you and people will remember that.

When we learn to stop looking at people to provide us with what can only come from God, we also learn that God will help us protect our integrity. It doesn't matter that we give everything to help others, or that these same people may let us down or all together ignore us. When our focus is not on people, but rather on the one who promises that He notices even a cup of water given to someone in his name, we discover that no matter how people react, our Heavenly Father always rewards.

Joseph was finally remembered and brought out of that prison, not just because he interpreted dreams, but because of who he was. The interpretations of the King's dreams could be trusted because Joseph's character could be trusted.

In our callings, sometimes all we will have left is holding onto God tightly. When the storms are all around you, when people who you considered to be your closest friends turn their backs on you, keeping your integrity and holding onto God tightly will sustain you to the end.

LEGACY OF JOSEPH

If Moses began his calling in a position of power in Egypt, then it was Joseph who completed his calling as Egypt's second most powerful leader, subject only to Pharaoh himself.

Once Joseph interpreted Pharaoh's prophetic dreams about the coming seven years of abundance, followed by seven years of drought, within that same day, he was released from prison. Pharaoh had placed him in a position of honor and authority to oversee the preparation for the coming drought. Talk about climbing the corporate ladder. It was more like taking the corporate elevator to the top. All in one day!

Joseph's life was changed, suddenly. Think about it. As quickly as Joseph went from the safety of his father's home into slavery, so now, just as quickly, he goes from being thrown into prison to suddenly given a position that would enable him to affect the lives of millions of people and many nations.

God desires that each of our lives would leave a legacy – a footprint on your world that would make an impact for generations to come.

Oh, you might not become a Joseph, Moses or King David, but even so, God's goal for your calling is to impact many generations of peoples' lives. If you believe that your calling is just some kind of God given credential that you carry in your back pocket and pull out from time to time to impress some people that you are a messenger of the Lord, then you really don't understand God's purpose for the called.

There is not one man or woman of God in the Bible who obeyed their divine calling and did not leave an impact and legacy for others to follow.

If you have a calling, it is because God wants you to change the world. But in order for this to take place, each of us called individuals must be ready for our "suddenly" moments. Every hero in Scripture had one.

Moses had his burning bush, David had his Samuel anointing, Gideon had his threshing floor messenger, and Mary had her visit from the angel, Gabriel. As you are faithfully working for the Lord, your moment will happen as well, that moment when God brings you into your legacy and your divine destiny.

In her book, <u>Expect a Move from God in Your Life… Suddenly!</u>, Joyce Meyer says:

"There is a word that I want to deposit in you through God's word that you can hang onto for the rest of your life, and I hope you never forget it. It is the word "suddenly!" Sometimes when you have lived with something in your life a long, long time, you get to the point that you can limp along with it and go on about your business at the same time. But God heard those prayers that you prayed about the situation, and He remembers them. SUDDENLY He can move in your life and deliver you in a way that will just amaze you. I believe we need to expect God to move SUDDENLY!"

Expect God to move SUDDENLY! I love that quote. God will move and open doors suddenly, if we are open to it and expect for it to happen.

Joseph never forgot the dreams of his youth. Therefore, when the suddenly moment happened for him, he was fit and ready for service. All he needed was a shower and shave and he was ready to meet the king!

The Bible says in 2 Timothy 4:2, "Preach the word; be prepared in season and out of season; correct, rebuke and encourage—with great patience and careful instruction."

This was Joseph in a nutshell. He expected his season to change at any moment and he was prepared, focused and ready for his suddenly moment. He knew it was coming, it was just a matter of when.

He didn't need any preparation time before meeting Pharaoh. He didn't need any therapy to overcome the trauma of isolation. In fact, Joseph was probably practicing and preparing for years on what he was going to say to Pharaoh once his suddenly moment came. He knew that prison was just a temporary setback and once that season of his life was over, he was ready to move on.

And this is the key to reaching your destiny in regard to your calling. You have to believe it so much that even in your darkest moments, those times when it seems that no answer is on the horizon, you know your suddenly moment could happen at any time.

The problem with many in ministry is that they miss those suddenly moments all the time. God brings a moment when He is about to release them into a new season in their destiny, and as quickly as it comes, it's gone. They weren't even aware that it was right in front of them.

How many individuals in ministry right now are waiting more for their retirement plan to kick in than their suddenly moment? Their legacy is glaring at them, straight in their face, yet because they have become so committed to just endure the work of the Lord, they missed their opportunity to make a lasting impact. It was a moment that God had designed just for them.

This was not the case with Joseph. We read in Genesis 41:39-43:

Then Pharaoh said to Joseph, "Since God has made all this known to you, there is no one so discerning and wise as you. You shall be in charge of my palace, and all my people are to submit to your orders. Only with respect to the throne will I be greater than you." So Pharaoh said to Joseph, "I hereby put you in charge of the whole land of Egypt." Then Pharaoh took his signet ring from his finger and put it on Joseph's finger. He dressed him in robes of fine linen and put a gold chain around his neck. He had him ride in a chariot as his second-in-command, and people shouted before him, "Make way!" Thus he put him in charge of the whole land of Egypt."

I think the reason why many called individuals miss their suddenly moments is because they keep on looking for those big events, those audible voices, those parted Red Seas that we see happening in other people's callings. We feel that others seem to be recipients of all the blessings and we're just over here fighting for a little relevance in the work God has given us to do.

Your suddenly moment doesn't just take place when some huge external "lightning bolt" moment or event shows up. Usually it is a series of smaller "suddenlies" that eventually lead you to the bigger open door. The important thing is to be continually in tune with the Holy Spirit. If you are not, when the Holy Spirit convicts you to make that phone call, or to visit that person, or to make that small change in your ministry, designed to lead you to your "suddenly" moment, you are in danger of missing it all together.

When we are in tune with the Holy Spirit, Jesus promised us in John 16:13 that He will "guide us into all truth." The important thing is to not only hear Him, but to be obedient to Him when He tells us to move.

In Chapter 8, I talk about a dream that the Lord gave me that would change the course of my ministry. If I had not been sensitive enough to know that the dream was from the Lord, I could have brushed it off as just an odd dream, thinking that it was nothing spiritual. Yet for me, one of my biggest suddenly moments happened with a dream!

Although the Bible doesn't tell us this, I really don't believe that the only dreams that Joseph had were the ones we read about. I honestly believe that while he was in prison, God continued to speak to Joseph through dreams and visions to encourage his heart and to help him keep his focus on the promised blessings.

In this story of Joseph, we read in Genesis 42:6-9a, how his family got word that there was food available in Egypt.

"Now Joseph was the governor of the land, the person who sold grain to all its people. So when Joseph's brothers arrived, they bowed down to him with their faces to the ground. As soon as Joseph saw his brothers, he recognized them, but he pretended to be a stranger and spoke harshly to them. "Where do you come from?" he asked. "From the land of Canaan," they replied, "to buy food." Although Joseph recognized his brothers, they did not recognize him. Then he remembered his dreams about them."

Joseph never forgot the dreams that the Lord gave him as a child. Although now older and wiser, he never strayed away from the purpose of his destiny. When he saw his brothers, the Bible tells us that he recognizes them and yet, probably because he was so young when he left home, they did not know who he was. As he looked at each of them, "he remembered his dreams about them."

Now please, don't miss the magnitude of what is happening at that moment. When Joseph saw these older brothers bowing down to him, the very ones who years earlier tried to kill him, Joseph suddenly had a flashback moment when he realized that God was now suddenly fulfilling his boyhood destiny.

We read that once he realized that his brothers didn't recognize him, Joseph took the time to test his brothers' character. Were they the same hostile siblings of so long ago? What about his father and his younger brother? Did they harm them like they had him? He now had their lives in the palm of his hand, and it was at this moment that his character was being tested, as much as theirs.

Although Joseph was seeing his destiny being fulfilled right before his very eyes, understand that even at this moment, Joseph still had the free will to destroy everything that the Lord had been building up to now.

He could have had each of his brothers executed on the spot, and perhaps feeling righteously justified for doing so, yet lose the very legacy that God wanted him to have.

When God begins to bless and fulfill our callings, when our suddenly moments seem to be happening right before our eyes, it is critical that you consciously protect yourself from the sin of pride and revenge. What I mean by this is, as you commit yourself to the calling and begin to see it fulfilled, you will be tempted in these areas.

A major area of temptation the devil uses at this moment is pride and revenge. You may be tempted to ridicule or speak ill of those who might have put stumbling blocks along your way. They could have been family members, like in Joseph's case. They could have been church members, fellow clergy, or any one. But, they were people who hurt you or didn't believe in you. Too often, without our even knowing it, Satan himself has used us to try to stifle our own calling.

When those thoughts of the past show up again and those feelings of hurt and betrayal rise up, you need to remember the truth. The truth is, you forgave them (right?). The truth is that it wasn't even them who did these things against you. It was the devil himself trying to prevent you from reaching your divine destiny and fulfilling your legacy. The truth is we wrestle not against flesh and blood. Don't let the enemy turn your focus from the truth onto the lies.

Joseph knew this very clearly. He knew that God had placed a great calling on his life, and Satan tried to use Joseph's own flesh and blood to stop Joseph's legacy before it even started. The ironic thing is that what Satan tried to use to destroy one person, Joseph, God used to save many!

We find in Genesis, Chapters 42-45, that before Joseph could reveal his identity to his brothers, he had to test their character.

First, he had them falsely accused of theft. Then he had them imprisoned for three days and then he had Simeon imprisoned until they went home and brought back their youngest brother, Benjamin. Joseph had the silver they paid for the grain with put back in their grain bags, which caused them to fear retribution if they returned to Egypt.

When starvation convinced Jacob to allow them to go back with Benjamin, Joseph tested their character even further by placing his silver cup in Benjamin's grain sack, only later to be found by Joseph's guards. Once the cup was discovered, Joseph vowed that young Benjamin would become an Egyptian slave for the rest of his life.

When he made this decree, Joseph then heard what he had been waiting to hear all along. For it was then that his brothers began to confess what they had done to Joseph so long ago. They pleaded that the same thing wouldn't happen to Benjamin in order to prevent their father, Jacob, from going through any more anguish.

With their true repentant character now exposed, Joseph knew that it was time to reveal not only his true identity, but also his destiny.

"Then Joseph said to his brothers, "Come close to me." When they had done so, he said, "I am your brother Joseph, the one you sold into Egypt! And now, do not be distressed and do not be angry with yourselves for selling me here, because it was to save lives that God sent me ahead of you. For two years now there has been famine in the land, and for the next five years there will be no plowing and reaping. But God sent me ahead of you to preserve for you a remnant on earth and to save your lives by a great deliverance. So then, it was not you who sent me here, but God. He made me father to Pharaoh, lord of his entire household and ruler of all Egypt. Now hurry back to my father and say to him, "This is what your son Joseph says: God has made me lord of all Egypt. Come down to me; don't delay. You shall live in the region of Goshen and be near me'" (Genesis 45:4-10a).

When we read about how Joseph tormented his brothers, he wasn't seeking revenge for what they had done to him. He was actually testing their hearts. He wanted to see if they were ready for their own suddenly moment or if they were still the revengeful group of men that he knew as a boy.

As Joseph had been blessed by God, he was about to pass that suddenly blessing onto his family as well. Their lives would be changed forever. Joseph knew exactly why he was sent to Egypt. As he told his brothers, "God sent me ahead of you to preserve for you a remnant on earth and to save your lives by a great deliverance." And, "it wasn't you who sent me here, but God."

Joseph's legacy was huge because he learned over the years to navigate through each storm that came his way, continuing on towards his destiny. Even though as a child his seemingly pampered ways caused him to be resented by his older siblings, in the end, even those moments were used to fulfill God's will for Joseph and the future nation of Israel.

We read in Genesis 50:24-26, years later, just before Joseph's death, he says to his brothers:

"I am about to die. But God will surely come to your aid and take you up out of this land to the land he promised on oath to Abraham, Isaac and Jacob." And Joseph made the Israelites swear an oath and said, "God will surely come to your aid, and then you must carry my bones up from this place." So Joseph died at the age of a hundred and ten. And after they embalmed him, he was placed in a coffin in Egypt."

Joseph was able to live long enough to understand God's ultimate plan of deliverance; that one day, a great gathering of people would arise from Jacob and his descendants. They would be a people that would eventually bring forth a new generation and a new leader named Moses who would help create a new nation, led by God Himself, that would change our world and eternity forever.

If you are called, it is because God has a divine legacy that He wants to give you that will long outlive your years on this earth. Your calling is not just for you. Your calling, if you are obedient to it, will raise up a host of servants of the Lord who were impacted by your obedience.

Joseph was so much a part of the Hebrews' DNA, that when the time finally came 300 years later for Moses to deliver the Hebrews from bondage, as we read in Exodus 13:19, "Moses took the bones of Joseph with him because Joseph had made the Israelites swear an oath. He had said, "God will surely come to your aid, and then you must carry my bones up with you from this place.""

I pray the same for you. I pray that your impact, your anointing, will be so effective, so powerful, so inspirational, that generations from now, people who never even met you would desire to "visit your bones" at some gravesite. They would say, "Because of this man, because of this woman, of God, because of their obedience to their calling, I am where I am today!"

CHAPTER 6

THE CALLING OF MOSES

LINEAGE OF MOSES

Let's move forward 300 hundred years to the Patriarch, Moses. When it comes to his lineage, we have to gather the information from a variety of Scriptures. For example, in Exodus 6, we find that Moses was the younger brother to Aaron. In Numbers 26, we find Moses' sister's name was Miriam, and their father's name was Amran, who married Jochebed, his father's sister. Interesting family dynamics to say the least.

Other than this, there's not much more to add. Even Moses' name wasn't given to him by his parents. Exodus 2:10 tell us that after Pharaoh's daughter found his basket floating amongst the bulrushes, she named him Moses (Moshe) saying, "I drew him out of the water."

Not much to go on, but truth is, I'm glad it's that way. I love the fact that the calling that God places on our lives has nothing to do with who we are related to. What a relief this is for so many!

I'm embarrassed to say that in my early years in ministry, I had a difficult time understanding this reality. I knew a number of my peers who quickly became successful pastors and ministry leaders, whose family names were quite well-known. As a young pastor, in my immaturity, I would jealously think that their ministry opportunities were only moving forward because of their famous last names.

Now that I am a bit older and wiser, I understand that a family name can, in some cases, actually be a hindrance and distraction to the calling. Comparisons can be unfairly made, and many a son and daughter of well-known spiritual leaders can find it frustrating living under the shadow of their family name.

I remember the first time I heard Franklin Graham preach at a crusade. Having grown up listening to his father's, Billy Graham, sermons for years, I began making comparisons of Franklin's preaching style to his father's. I thought to myself that I enjoyed Billy's preaching much better. However, Franklin is a powerful speaker and his passion for world evangelism would be difficult to duplicate. If I had not known that he was Billy Graham's son, I would not have made that comparison and would have been impressed from the moment I heard him.

The success of his ministry, Samaritan's Purse, had nothing to do with his father's name. Rather, it speaks of Franklin's own personality and God-given giftings to take the dream that God gave him and make it a reality.

The fact that he is Billy's son only reminds me that God's word is true, as we see in Proverbs 22:6 (NKJV), "Train up a child in the way he should go, and when he is old he will not depart from it."

I see this clearly now, but back in the early 90's, when I was just starting out in ministry, my thinking was much more limited and naïve. One time I was listening to a tape in my car of John Maxwell that my senior pastor asked me to listen to. Yes, a tape; I did say it was the early 90's! In this tape, John Maxwell was speaking on "People of Influence." In the message, he said, "Much of my success I can base upon the life of this man sitting right here, my father."

I thought to myself, "Well, no wonder he is so successful, he had a great dad who probably opened some huge doors for him." That thought barely had the chance to percolate in my mind when the Lord suddenly interrupted my pity party and said, "I thought you gave that to Me? Why are you digging that garbage back up?"

Tears began to fill up in my eyes as I realized that once again I was digging up old feelings that I needed to be kept crucified. I quickly spoke out verbally, "Jesus, I'm sorry. I realize that my success in my calling has nothing to do who my dad was, but rather who my Heavenly Father is." I never forgot that moment, even though over 25 years have passed since then.

Your success in ministry will never base itself upon whom you are related to. Oh, it might help you open that first door, but truth be known, after that, unless the anointing is IN you and the calling is ON you, your success will quickly stall out.

INDIVIDUALITY

Anyone who has a special calling on their life, in very unique ways has their own individuality. Now, I understand that everyone of us in the world is uniquely created by God. There has never been or ever will be another 'you' created in this world, but that's not what I'm talking about here.

What I want to stress here is that when it comes to a called individual, their uniqueness sets them apart from the crowd. They are, as I said in Chapter 3, the square peg in the round hole, and it has everything to do with being set apart for the Lord's work.

Moses himself was unique. Can you imagine the family functions that Moses had with his adopted relatives? How many times do you think that his discovery as an infant was the topic around the family dinner table? Moses understood his uniqueness. He understood that he was different than everyone else in the royal family. Yet his unique qualities had nothing to do with whom his family or lineage was, but had everything to do with what was inside of him.

DEFINING THE CALL

As far as Moses' background goes, he definitely didn't have an Abraham as a great grandfather or an Isaac as a grandfather. Jacob definitely was not standing by his side to give him fatherly wisdom and advice like Joseph had as a child. Yet what Moses did have was God's anointing and protection all over him, and this was proven the moment he was born.

The same God who protected him from Pharaoh's murderous plots and the hungry Nile crocodiles, is the same God who would lead him to his called destiny.

Although the Bible is quiet about Moses' father, we do know that he was loved by his mother, Jochebed, who saw that this baby was someone special. When Pharaoh was determined to destroy all the Hebrew boys out of fear that his throne would be overtaken by a Hebrew slave coup, his mother had the faith in God and passion to save her child at any cost, even at the cost of her own life.

In Exodus 2:2a-4, we read, "When she saw that he was a fine child, she hid him for three months. But when she could hide him no longer, she got a papyrus basket for him and coated it with tar and pitch. Then she placed the child in it and put it among the reeds along the bank of the Nile. His sister stood at a distance to see what would happen to him."

God had placed Moses in the Hebrew/Levite family of a mother who saw him for what he was, "a fine child." She couldn't offer him any material wealth, she couldn't even promise to spare his life. All she could do was release him to the Lord and pray that the Lord's hand would be upon him.

Once my father was gone, our home environment changed dramatically. The tension was gone, but so was the stability of a main income. Mom didn't have much to offer us, but she did have her faith in the Lord.

I clearly remember the day when I was about 15 years of age, I was in a low place emotionally and my mother knew it. She came into my room and opened up her Bible to Psalm 68:5 and read, "A father to the fatherless, a

The Calling of Moses

defender of widows, is God in His holy dwelling."

She said with a confidence that I'll never forget, "Your dad is gone, but God promises that He will be your father, and He will be my defender." After reading those words, she stood there looking in my eyes, hoping that I understood the reality of what she just read.

She was unable to offer me any financial security. She had no money, nor did she have any costly family heirloom in her hands to give to me. But what she was offering me at that moment was what Jochebed did for her baby, Moses. She was releasing me out into the will of God, into the Nile of an ungodly world where the spiritual attacks of Satan's "crocodiles" laid in wait.

In telling me that God was going to be a father to me, it began to teach me, in some small way, that the uniqueness of my family situation was what God would use to prepare me for a unique calling. That I, like Moses, was placed in very unique circumstances where the odds were stacked against me. And like Moses, God's divine guidance would direct my path through the currents of life's challenges right into His divine plan for my future.

For every unique testimony creates very unique people, who many times are called to very unique ministries.

In his papyrus basket, sealed with pitch and tar, God led baby Moses to safety and into the loving arms of Pharaoh's daughter. For the next 40 years, he was raised as an Egyptian prince, yet, never forgetting his roots. He had everything he wanted when it came to the luxuries of the ancient world, yet deep within his heart, he knew that he was different.

Although he wore their clothing, ate their food and spoke their language, he knew he didn't fit in. Not socially, not culturally and definitely not spiritually. I am sure many times he wondered who the mother was that released him as an infant into the Nile. And, each time he saw a Hebrew slave, there was something deep within him, something unexplainable that drew him to these foreign people.

This is where we see the next, and probably the most powerful and revealing, attribute of the called.

COMPASSION

I want you to imagine with me the situation. Here is one of the most powerful men in all of Egypt watching this city being built, mostly under his supervision and direction. One day he sees one of his fellow Hebrews being beaten by an Egyptian guard.

Now understand, these people were slaves. They didn't have the rights and privileges of the average person, and whippings and beatings of slaves was an every day occurrence in that culture. Yet, when Moses saw this slave being beaten, a righteous anger burned within him that started a fire.

This wasn't like he was witnessing a street mugging of an innocent victim that needed rescuing. What Moses was observing, to the average Egyptian official, should have been as unassuming and uninteresting as someone hitting a disobedient dog. But, not for Moses. Something happened inside of him that day that changed his life forever.

Out of all the hundreds of beatings of slaves that Moses witnessed over the years, when he saw this one, it was like he was witnessing every beating that he saw up until then happening all at once. His righteous anger and compassion could not hold back any longer. He decided once and for all, at that very moment, enough is enough. He was going to do something about it.

"Looking this way and that and seeing no one, he killed the Egyptian and hid him in the sand. The next day he went out and saw two Hebrews fighting. He asked the one in the wrong, "Why are you hitting your fellow Hebrew?" The man said, "Who made you ruler and judge over us? Are you thinking of killing me as you killed the Egyptian?" Then Moses was afraid and thought, "What I did must have become known." When Pharaoh heard of this, he tried to kill Moses, but Moses fled from Pharaoh and went to live in Midian where he sat down by a well" (Exodus 2:12-15).

It was this decision, a "suddenly moment," that changed his life forever. From this point on, he was no longer the man of royalty and power that he had just been a few moments earlier. He was now a fugitive, a man running for his life, yet inside, I am sure he never felt so free and liberated as he did at that moment.

Moses no longer had to hide his true identity. The passion that he had for his fellow Hebrews could now be expressed and used to finally deliver them from their bondage. You think that God would have taken Moses right at that moment, turned him on his heels right back to that heartless Pharaoh and tell him, "Let my people go!" Yet, God knew better. He understood that despite Moses' zeal and compassion, he still needed some time for nurturing and development. Forty more years to be exact. We will look at this further in "Lessons of Moses."

The one attribute that every called individual will always need is compassion. It is the one thing that sets them apart from so many others. It is also the one thing that when it is lost, so is their entire ministry.

Paul writes in Colossians 3:12, "Therefore, as God's chosen people, holy and dearly loved, clothe yourselves with compassion, kindness, humility, gentleness and patience."

Compassion, along with all the other attributes mentioned here, needs to be so much a part of who we are that they are like Joseph's coat of many colors. These attributes should be so evidently wrapped around one's soul that everyone notices and admires them.

Moses' compassion was more than just having pity on this helpless Hebrew slave. It was much deeper than that. The compassion that Moses possessed was a selfless compassion. It was compassion like that of Jesus, who gave without expecting anything in return.

If the situation were reversed and Moses was saving the life of an Egyptian official who was being attacked by a slave, one might argue that he was only saving their life for selfish motives. Perhaps, that in helping them, they would be able to return the favor to Moses down the road. But that wasn't the case with this scenario. This slave could offer nothing to Moses in return. He was just a beast of burden to the average Egyptian, yet in Moses' eyes, he was a fellow Hebrew. Moses was willing to help, despite the danger that his own livelihood could be in jeopardy. Moses was a man of great character and as the saying goes, great character can be seen in how you treat those who can do nothing for you.

The person with the calling needs to allow the Holy Spirit to continually instill in them this type of compassion. Compassion with no strings attached. Without it, there is absolutely no hope that their divine calling will ever see any major success.

Many spiritual leaders have lost their compassion for people. They no longer see people as souls who have a destiny with God, but rather, they perceive them as tools and pawns for the leader's greater good.

If a person has talents, gifts or training that could benefit one's ministry, then guaranteed, the visits will take place, the accolades will be given and the compassion will flow. But, if the individual seems more of a nuisance than a help, more of a liability than a benefit, then compassion is limited or all together ignored.

Inventor and botanist, George Washington Carver once said this about compassion:

"How far you go in life depends on your being tender with the young, compassionate with the aged, sympathetic with the striving and tolerant of the weak and strong. Because someday in your life you will have been all of these."

The questions you need to ask yourself, over and over again, are, "How is my compassion?" "Is it where it was when I first felt God's calling on my life?" "Am I just as enthusiastic in reaching the lost today as I was last year, or a month ago or even yesterday?" If you are hesitant, even just a little, in answering a resounding YES, then you need to realign your compassion with the purpose of what your calling means to you.

Unconditional, genuine compassion is the one thing that will set you apart from other so called spiritual leaders who may be involved in the work of the Lord for the wrong reasons.

It was Theodore Roosevelt who was quoted as saying, "People don't care about how much you know until they know how much you care."

The one thing that set Jesus apart from the Rabbis and Pharisees of his day was not necessarily what He taught, but rather how He taught it. He gave the Word as if it were alive. The truth is, it is alive. "Jesus was the Word." (See John 1:14.)

Jesus' compassion was so real that when He taught the Scriptures it was as if His audience was receiving it through all five of their senses. Those who believed in Jesus did so because they sensed His compassion towards them was real and was flowing from God Himself.

A main reason why Moses was chosen for the task of delivering the Hebrew slaves was because of his compassion. His love for these people was so evident that in Numbers 14 we read how he stood between God and the Hebrews when God was about to destroy them because of their rebellion. Pleading with God, Moses begged God to spare their lives, even though these were the same people who just minutes earlier wanted to kill Moses himself.

This type of love is highly rare. It's the type of love and compassion that Jesus was speaking of in John 15:13 (KJV), "Greater love hath no man than this, that a man lay down his life for his friends."

There was no possible way that Moses could have ever survived those 40 years in the desert with these people if he didn't have a supernatural compassion for them. No normal leadership skill set could have accomplished what God was calling Moses to do. No set of social skills that the world may offer can maintain your calling either.

LESSONS OF MOSES

Out of the three patriarchs that we are discussing, when it comes to Moses, the lessons that we can glean from his life are many, to say the least. Just his life alone, his ministry, and the many incredible stories while in the wilderness could probably fill an entire book on lessons for the called. Yet for the benefit of this book, I'd like to focus on five very powerful lessons that each called individual needs to pay attention to.

WALK IN GOD'S TIMING, NOT YOUR OWN

After fleeing Egypt, the Bible tells us that Moses fled to the desert of Midian where he came into contact with the seven daughters of Jethro, who was a Midianite priest. They were watering their sheep and goats by a well and Moses stopped there to rest.

After witnessing some other shepherds forcing their way to the well before Jethro's daughters were finished, Moses once again stepped in to save the day and protected them from this unruly lot. For his heroic deeds, Moses was then invited by the young ladies to meet their father.

As the story goes, their father was so impressed with this young man that he offers his daughter, Zipporah, to Moses as his wife. Over time, she gave him two sons, Gershom and Eliezer. For the next 40 years, we really don't hear anything about what happened in Moses' life until we finally find him at Mt. Horeb hearing from God through the burning bush. (See Acts 7:23-30.)

Did you catch that? Forty years! I don't know about you, but 40 years to me seems like a long time. I mean, what was I doing 40 years ago? Well, I was 12 years of age, and at that age, all I was concerned about was building my tree fort and hanging out with my buddies after school!

Waiting on God to make His next big move in our lives is never easy. Just like Joseph before him, there was a waiting period Moses had to endure before his suddenly moment at the burning bush came along. But the key to it all was that Moses had to be ready for it. No matter how long it took and no matter how hum-drum his present circumstances may have seemed, Moses needed to be listening to God's voice at any moment.

Moses' waiting period was really for two reasons. Just like Joseph, there was a bit of humbling that needed to be worked into Moses' character. His early years of living with the Egyptian royal family no doubt gave him opportunities for education and affluence that his fellow Hebrews could only dream of. In Acts 7:22 we read that, "Moses was given the best education in Egypt. He was a strong man and a powerful speaker," and yet in Exodus 4:10, after 40 years living as a shepherd, Moses says to the Lord, "I have never been a good speaker. I wasn't one before you spoke to me, and I'm not one now. I am slow at speaking, and I can never think of what to say."

What happened to the Moses described in Acts 7 and the man we witness in Exodus 4? I'll tell you what happened. Forty years happened! Moses was definitely a different man at 80 years of age than he was at 40. He was humbled, tried and tested. Now, 40 years later, he was ready for his suddenly moment, even though he himself felt inadequate by this time.

As the 40 years was definitely for Moses' development and maturing, we can also see that this 40-year period also served the purpose of preparing God's people to become a people who would be ready and desperate for a deliverer. We see this in Exodus 2:23-25 (emphasis added):

"During that LONG PERIOD, the king of Egypt died. The Israelites groaned in their slavery and cried out, and their cry for help because of their slavery went up to God. God heard their groaning and he remembered His covenant with Abraham, with Isaac and with Jacob. So God looked on the Israelites and was concerned about them."

In these verses we can see that two things had to happen before Moses could ever deliver the Hebrew slaves from their misery. First, a new Pharaoh had to come to the throne, and second, God's people had to be desperate.

As God leads us in our callings, we must always allow the Lord to lead our steps forward and always do our best to not force His hand. His plans for us far surpass our own in what we can imagine or hope for. The key to this blessing is always timing.

We see this again in Acts 16 when the Apostle Paul was forbidden by the Holy Spirit to minister in Asia and Bithynia. It didn't mean that God didn't want the gospel to reach that area, but for some reason, it wasn't the right timing.

Like Paul, we need to always be sensitive and alert for the Holy Spirit's leading and to understand that God's ways and His timing are not always ours. Like Joseph waiting in prison for his suddenly moment, Moses too had to wait for his for 40 years while he raised his family in his father-in-law's household. Waiting and preparing, while both his character and the political situation in Egypt met head on at just the right moment.

Far too many who are called, out of a determination to succeed in the work of the Lord, try to force things to happen when they want it to happen rather than waiting on the Lord.

Successful ministries, as God sees them, along with divine moves of the Lord, always work under the premise that all the elements come together at the moment of God's perfect timing. If Moses had gone back to Egypt before God's will, it would have been a colossal failure. The wrong Pharaoh would have been in power, the Hebrew people would have not been ready for a deliverer, and Moses' actions would have looked more like a political coup to overthrow Pharaoh rather than a divine deliverance of God's people.

He would have had no divine authority. No plagues sent by God, no staff turning into a snake, no Passover angel and certainly no parting of the Red Sea.

The Calling of Moses

Joyce Meyer says, in her <u>Ending Your Day Right</u> devotional, the following about timing:

"God moves in his timing not yours. He is never late, but He is usually not early either. He is often the God of the midnight hour. He sometimes waits until the last second before He gives you what you need. Before He intervenes on your behalf, He has to be sure you are not going to take matters into your own hands and do something out of His perfect timing. You must learn to trust God's timing. But first your self-will and your spirit of independence must be broken so that God is free to work His will in your life and circumstances. If you are waiting for something, set aside your own timetable tonight. Trust God and believe that while you are waiting for your breakthrough, He is doing a good work in you for His purpose."

The called man and woman of God will always need to be sensitive to God's perfect timing. To go when God says go, to wait when God says wait, and avoid altogether when God says no.

This discernment will be critical for the called, especially when you have people in leadership around you who are more swayed and influenced by public opinion rather than the will of God. This is not to say that the called should not lean on the opinion of others. Scripture is very clear on this. What it does mean is that at the end of the day, you must undeniably know and understand that the decision that you made is from God and not one that is made because it is the most popular decision or makes the best business sense.

Moses waited. For 40 years he waited. Yet, when he finally moved forward, He knew that he was in the direct and exact will of God!

"GO FOR NO."

My wife has worked for a very successful real estate firm for the last number of years. One thing that the agents are taught is a term that originated from Richard Fenton and Andrea Waltz, which is "Go For No."

Basically, what this means is that failing and failure are two very different things. It is vitally important that each of us celebrate our success as well as our failures. The key to success is how we get past failures quickly and move on from there. The most empowering word in the world is not yes; it's no! 'Yes' is the destination and 'No' is how you get there! Learn what you need to learn from your No, and press on towards your eventual Yes!

I couldn't agree more with this perspective. And, it relates so much to the story of Moses.

Have you ever thought of what was going through the minds of Moses and Aaron when they were confronting Pharaoh in challenging him to let God's people go?

When they first challenged Pharaoh to free the Hebrew slaves, Pharaoh responds by making the slaves work even harder and forcing them to gather their own straw to make the clay bricks. His response was a definite, "No!"

When Moses and Aaron approached Pharaoh for the second time, Aaron throws his staff to the ground as God commanded and it became a snake, only to discover that Pharaoh's magicians could do the same. Granted, Aarons staff ate theirs, but still a bit deflating that these magicians were able to do the same stick to snake trick as them.

Then God commanded Moses to turn the water to blood, and it says in Exodus 7:20-21 that when Aaron's staff "struck the water of the Nile, and all the water was changed into blood. The fish in the Nile died, and the river smelled so bad that the Egyptians could not drink its water. Blood was everywhere in Egypt." In verse 22 we see, "But the Egyptian magicians did the same thing by their secret arts, and Pharaoh's heart became hard; he would not listen to Moses and Aaron." Pharaoh's response, again, was a definite, "No!"

The important lesson to glean from what is going on in this story is the fact that being used by the Lord in a calling is not a life of providing supernatural magic tricks and impressive performances to get peoples' attention.

Far too many people in ministry have fallen for the façade or delusion of performing God's work, rather than being His messenger. For many ministries out there, when you truly get to the core of what it is that they are trying to accomplish, it is nothing more than a form of entertainment that is attempting to build their own name rather than the Kingdom of God.

When ministry becomes something that is competing with the world, the work of God will always lose out. We are not trying to impress the world with what we are offering, because we are not offering a product or experience, but rather, we are giving a message; the only message! And it is this message of hope and salvation that not only promises to stimulate the five senses, but also to impact our entire body, soul and spirit and to realign us with a right relationship with our Creator.

When we receive opposition and the "No" like Moses and Aaron did, we should not be at all surprised. Moses and his brother were symbolically standing right at the gates of hell itself when they were demanding the release of God's people. They were taking back what Satan had stolen and Satan knew that his grip on this ordained nation of God was about to be broken. So, no magic trick, no smoke show, was going to convince the heart of this evil ruler to change his mind.

If anything, I believe that when God performs these supernatural feats before our eyes, they are there more to encourage the heart of God's messenger than to convince the spiritually lost that the message is true.

Each time that Moses came to Pharaoh and released the plagues on the people of Egypt, the faith of Moses and Aaron were strengthened. Each time they got the empty promises back from Pharaoh that he would allow the slaves to be released, only to change his mind, Moses' spirit was more emboldened.

Why? Because when he saw God sending the blood in the water, when he saw plagues of frogs, the flies, the boils, the locusts, the plague of darkness, and everything else that God brought upon them, he was encouraged. No doubt it caused incredible anguish for the people of Egypt, but what it did even more was let Moses and Aaron know to keep on pushing, because their God was working through them.

In your calling, expect to hear No! Expect the rejection and the spiritual warfare. But also, expect the eventual deliverance for those who keep pushing and praying through.

I don't recall where I saw this, but John Maxwell said, "Ninety percent of those who fail are not actually defeated; they simply quit. As you face bad experiences, it's important for you to remember that you can rarely see the benefits while you're in the midst of them. You usually gain perspective on the other side of it."

When you "Go For No," you expect that you will experience moments of rejection, moments of frustration, times of opposition. But remember, Yes is the destination, No is how you get there. Because Moses and Aaron saw that God was with them, their focus was not on the No from Pharaoh, but rather on the eventual Yes from God who would provide for them if they remained committed.

Question: When did Pharaoh finally fully commit to release God's people from Egypt? The answer is: When his own personal life was affected. When the Passover angel touched each family in Egypt by killing the first-born male in each household that did not have the lamb's blood over their doorposts, and when Pharaoh's own household was affected, it was only then that Pharaoh's stubborn will was broken.

At midnight, when Pharaoh found his only son dead by this final plague, he knew he wasn't dealing with just a couple of crazed old men that could preform some impressive magic tricks. Pharaoh understood, at that moment, that he was dealing with the Hebrew God that had the power over life and death.

Your calling will only be in the midst of God's will when you commit yourself to presenting a message that goes straight to the heart of peoples' lives and eternal destiny. We will never change our world by entertaining them. The lost will never choose to come to the Lord because your magic show was more impressive and inspiring than the world's.

The church of North America has tried this for years, and it has failed miserably in this endeavor. But when you stand your ground, expecting and accepting to hear No and the rejection that comes with presenting the whole aspect of the gospel message, which includes the issue of sin, then, and only then, will your ministry be effective and worth the hardships that will come against you.

GO DEEP WITH GOD – EVEN WHEN YOU HAVE TO GO ALONE

I would like to spend a little more time on this third lesson of Moses' due to the important fact that this was a major part of who Moses was called to be. Moses' calling was not just to lead a group of people from slavery to the Promised Land. In actuality, Moses' calling was to build the moral foundation that would affect not only the future nation of Israel, but also countless future nations around the world. The commandments of morality and truth, the Ten Commandments, would become the very foundation, the very footing, in which many Judeo-Christian cultures would become established. God meeting with Moses at that sacred mountain was not only birthing a nation, but also establishing the moral absolutes that many secular people just take for granted. It is a foundation of right and wrong.

After living off the high of the release of God's people, I am sure Moses felt that he could accomplish absolutely anything. I mean, just imagine it. In Exodus 12:31-32a, Pharaoh finally says to Moses and Aaron, "Up! Leave my people, you and the Israelites! Go, worship the Lord as you have requested. Take your flocks and herds, as you have said, and go."

After hearing No for so long, finally their Yes came true! And not just that, but they got the loot as well! In verses 35-36, we read, "The Israelites did as Moses instructed and asked the Egyptians for articles of silver and gold and for clothing. The Lord had made the Egyptians favorably disposed toward the people, and they gave them what they asked for; so they plundered the Egyptians."

It's an amazing feeling when you see God doing the miraculous right before your very eyes. When doors that you have prayed for years to open suddenly swing wide, and you're almost in a state of shock and can hardly believe what you are witnessing, it is a most amazing experience.

I remember standing before my congregation one Sunday in 2012, giving them the news that the land that we owned for over a decade was finally now able to sell for way more than we paid for it. After years of one obstacle after another, one fallen through offer after another, government expropriations, you name it, our land was finally sold and we now had the opportunity to take some amazing steps forward. These were steps that our congregation, up until then, could only dream of. It was a great feeling, a wonderful accomplishment! Yet, in the midst of all this celebration, I felt an uneasiness, a restless feeling in the back of my mind that was warning me of a coming storm. It was almost like Moses leading the parade of the free Israelite children, filled with joy and euphoria, and then hearing a concerning distant rumble, unaware that Egyptian horses and chariots were advancing upon them to steal back their freedom and deliverance.

After sharing this wonderful news with my church, I suddenly felt compelled to say something that wasn't a part of my announcement. I said, "I know that we are all excited about this moment that we have been waiting for and praying for so long, and we should be. But, I need to give each of us a clear warning. Expect the attacks. Expect that Satan will do everything in his power to destroy the blessing that is before us. Let us be diligent and watchful for his deceitful plans. Because he knows what God wants to do in this place, and he will do everything in his power to stop it."

I had no idea why I felt compelled to say this, and I certainly had no idea how difficult and large the storm would be that awaited us. Without getting into the details, within a year of this blessing, the spiritual attacks our congregation went through were incredibly intense. Bringing division between friends and family, this situation was a clear physical manifestation of God separating the wheat from the chaff, which is never a pleasant experience.

In the end, true colors were exposed and the dark intentions of the wolves in sheep's clothing were revealed. Yet looking back, it is now easy to see how God used trials like these to launch our family and my calling into a new chapter for God's work. What the devil meant for evil, God definitely was able to use for good. As you are faithful to your calling, the victories will be many.

Over the course of years, God will many times part the waters in your ministry, which will happen because of your determination and commitment to Him. Those moments are euphoric, and they are a gift from the Lord that He wants you to celebrate. Yet always remember, as with Moses, those who are patting you on your back, saying what a wonderful job you did in this milestone, might be the very ones who will be attacking your very character tomorrow.

Moses was now reaping the rewards for his faithfulness to the Lord. It wasn't easy. It was probably quite frightening for him, and probably extremely intimidating, to stand up to Pharaoh the way he did. Yet God's promises to Israel were now being fulfilled and the doors facing east towards the Promised Land stood wide open. They were miraculously guided by God with His pillar of cloud by day and pillar of fire by night. Everything seemed to be going the way it was supposed to go. Then came the Red Sea!

Once the Israelites began to see the Egyptian army advancing upon them, it didn't take long for those praises and the partying atmosphere to suddenly turn into cursing and complaining towards Moses.

"They said to Moses, "Was it because there were no graves in Egypt that you brought us to the desert to die? What have you done to us by bringing us out of Egypt? Didn't we say to you in Egypt, 'Leave us alone; let us serve the Egyptians'? It would have been better for us to serve the Egyptians than to die in the desert!'" (See Exodus 14:11-12.)

I have always been amazed by this part of the story where Moses responds to these turncoat whiners that were just singing his praises seconds earlier. Maybe because every time I read it my mind goes straight to the movie with Charlton Heston who played Moses in the movie, "The Ten Commandments." But whatever image appears in my mind's eye, one thing we notice here is Moses' confidence and authority as he stands there before this sea of people looking to Him for answers. After he cries out to the Lord for help, God gives him the go ahead to tell the people to move out toward the sea. As Moses stretches out his hands over the water, the waters split in two.

Wow. What authority, what power, especially coming from a man who just months earlier was taking care of his father-in-law's herds.

I may be a bit off here, but I don't think so. I honestly believe that when Moses saw the waters before him, he had no doubt that God had a divine plan in mind. Think of it. He just came off an experience where he saw the hand of God move through his and Aaron's authority. These ten plagues were not any less spectacular than what they were about to experience at the Red Sea. The entire nation of Egypt came to a grinding halt because these huge catastrophes, which were so intense they even caused the death of many firstborn males.

Moses lived through all of those experiences and was now standing before the Red Sea. I believe that he was thinking that this was just the next one on the list for him. You would say that Moses was in the zone!

When you have those moments when God very actively and publicly is working through you, when the ministries are humming, when the services are anointed, when the sick are being healed, when the budgets are surpassed, there is a spiritual confidence that develops in those called. It's only natural, and it's part of the blessing. But one must always keep in mind that no matter how far you have come, you must always go back to the spiritual well to be refreshed. You need to be reminded of who you are, and who you were when you first felt that calling.

It could have been very easy for Moses to look at all that was happening through him and think that he was the man. But, that's not what we see. Somehow, Moses was able to separate himself from what God was doing through him. He never forgot that he was just the messenger and that God, and God alone, was the miracle maker.

You have all heard the old adage that says, "You can't give what you don't have." When it comes to the called, you will never be able to give and teach what you yourself haven't been given by God.

For me, up until recently, it has been well over 18 years since I actually sat under another pastor's ministry. As a shepherd, I have had to give, and give, and give the message Sunday after Sunday, praying that each and every time it is anointed and received straight from the Father heart of God.

I would not have been able to do this over and over again if I had not been going back to the well for His refreshing, and spending time alone every day with God, reflecting on who I am, the messenger, and that He, and He alone, is the miracle maker.

As called individuals, we cannot give, we cannot pour out, if we ourselves are not being filled. After 400 years of bondage, Moses was called to lead an entire nation of people out of slavery towards the Promised Land. When you discover how insecure and unqualified Moses initially felt about this, you begin to wonder how this feat was even possible in the first place.

To be called is never something that the person ever feels qualified for. If they do feel qualified for the calling, then this basically proves that they have no idea what they are getting themselves into.

Moses had five excuses that he laid before the Lord as to why he felt unable to fulfill this initial calling.

1. I'm not good enough! "But Moses said to God, "Who am I that I should go to Pharaoh and bring the Israelites out of Egypt?" Exodus 3:11

2. I don't have all the answers! "Moses said to God, "Suppose I go to the Israelites and say to them, 'The God of your fathers has sent me to you,' and they ask me, 'What is his name?' Then what shall I tell them?" Exodus 3:13

3. People won't believe me! "Moses answered, "What if they do not believe me or listen to me and say, 'The Lord did not appear to you'?" Exodus 4:1

4. I'm a terrible public speaker! "Moses said to the Lord, "Pardon your servant, Lord. I have never been eloquent, neither in the past nor since you have spoken to your servant. I am slow of speech and tongue." Exodus 4:10

5. I'm not qualified! "But Moses said, "Pardon your servant, Lord. Please send someone else." Exodus 4:13

I don't know about you, but when I read each of these excuses, I guarantee you that I have felt and experienced every last one of them!

As leaders, we are called to do just that, lead. We are called to have vision, passion and incredible faith to believe that our God can do anything.

Moses did not have this confidence in himself, and that is what made him such an incredible leader. Moses knew that anything that he was going to accomplish for these people had to come from God, because in himself, Moses could accomplish nothing.

Once the people of Israel were safely across the Red Sea, seeing that God had held back their enemies with the angel of God and the pillar of cloud until every last Israelite was safely across, Exodus 15 says that Moses and Aaron led the entire people in a song of praise.

Can you imagine being there when over a million delivered Hebrew men, women, boys and girls began to sing a song unto the Lord? What a sight to behold.

Yet something more important was revealed by this image of this million plus choir. It was a show of unity! It is recorded in Exodus 14:31, "And when the Israelites saw the mighty hand of the Lord displayed against the Egyptians, the people feared the Lord and put their trust in him and in Moses his servant."

Two things happened as a result of the Red Sea crossing. Without these two things, this journey out of Egypt would have failed right from the very first day. It says, "The people feared the Lord and trusted His servant Moses."

This should always be the goal for every called man and woman. Our goal is not that people follow us, but that through our faith and confidence in the Lord's deliverance, that in the end, their faith in God is strengthened, and their trust in us to continue in our role is reassured and enhanced.

The Bible says that once they crossed the Red Sea, God then quickly directed them to Mt. Sinai. It was one thing to physically save this mob of people from their years of depravity, but now it was time to begin to make them into the nation of God that He ordained for them to be. God had removed them from Egypt, but now He needed to remove Egypt from them.

When we think about Mt. Sinai and Moses, most of us automatically think of that moment when he met with God at the mountain summit and was given the Ten Commandments. Yet when you look at Scripture, you discover that there are at least eight recorded moments between Exodus 19 to 34 when Moses climbed up that high mountain to meet with the Lord and prepare this young nation for the Mosaic laws that God commanded.

I want to hone in on a few aspects of what was going on as it relates to Moses' relationship with God's people, Israel.

As God's servant, it was his responsibility to hear from the Lord and obey everything God commanded him to do.

In Exodus 19:9-13, upon immediately arriving at the base of Mount Sinai, Moses climbs the mountain to hear from the Lord. Initially by himself, he stands before the Lord as God says:

"I am going to come to you in a dense cloud, so that the people will hear me speaking with you and will always put their trust in you." Then Moses told the Lord what the people had said. And the Lord said to Moses, "Go to the people and consecrate them today and tomorrow. Have them wash their clothes and be ready by the third day, because on that day the Lord will come down on Mount Sinai in the sight of all the people. Put limits for the people around the mountain and tell them, 'Be careful that you do not approach the mountain or touch the foot of it. Whoever touches the mountain is to be put to death. They are to be stoned or shot with arrows; not a hand is to be laid on them. No person or animal shall be permitted to live.' Only when the ram's horn sounds a long blast may they approach the mountain."

Up to this point, the Israelites had no concept of who their God really was, nor what His expectations were of them.

As we saw, the Lord commands Moses to have the people, "Wash their clothes and be ready by the third day, because on that day the Lord will come down on Mount Sinai in the sight of all the people."

For the person who has a calling, your first responsibility, your first duty, is this: Express to your listeners and followers God's desire to be united with humanity!

Like Moses, who stood as a mediator between God and His people, Israel, our role is to take on that mediator or that arbitrator role, if we can call it that, between those we oversee and Jesus. Many church leaders make the leap to first show people their sin before they show them the grace of God. We see very clearly here in Exodus 19, that God tells Moses to first prepare the people to get themselves ready to meet with God.

Notice that God doesn't initially demand for Moses to make a blood sacrifice before they come to the mountain. Rather, the first thing that God tell Moses is, "Have them wash up and clean their clothes, because on the third day I am coming down in the sight of the people." What is God trying to teach the people of Israel here?

Well, just imagine with me that you get a call from your parents that they are coming over to see their grandkids. As soon as you hang up the phone, you quickly tell the children, "Okay, get ready, put on your clean clothes, wash up because Grandma and Grandpa are coming over."

God first gives Moses the invitation for the people to prepare for his visit, and then He says the following, "Put limits for the people around the mountain and tell them, 'Be careful that you do not approach the mountain or touch the foot of it. Whoever touches the mountain is to be put to death.'"

In other words, to use the grandma and grandpa analogy again, it's like your kids getting all cleaned up to see their grandparents and yet, when they come in the door, your children are told that they are not allow to hug them or get near them or they will be punished.

God, right away, was teaching Israel a lesson. He is saying, "I want to be near you, I desire to dwell with you, but there is a problem, it's called sin."

For the next 15 chapters in Exodus, and over 40 days, we find Moses going up and down that sacred mountain. And while he was up there, Moses received from the Lord the Ten Commandments, the Laws of the Torah, the guidelines to the tabernacle sacrificial system, as well as how to live as a nation under God's moral guidance.

Embedded throughout all of these laws was the basic reality that God is holy and that man is not. Unlike the teachings they were influenced by in the Egyptian culture that taught that Pharaoh himself was a god, the true God of Israel was now revealing to Israel that all of creation was tarnished by sin and was in desperate need of God's intervention. That, "without the shedding of blood there is no forgiveness." (See Hebrews 9:22b.)

For many years after Moses' Mt. Sinai experience, Israel's continual repetition of the Holy Feasts and sacrifices for hundreds of years taught them that, "It is impossible for the blood of bulls and goats to take away sin" (Hebrews 10:4). It taught them that the holy days, like Yom Kipper (Day of Atonement), were only a type, a reminder, that one day God would intervene and do away with the curse of sin once and for all.

As leaders, like Moses, we are called to climb that mountain on a regular basis towards the presence of God, to seek His leading and guidance. It's not always easy and it takes discipline, but without it, you will always fall short of the anointing that God has for you. You can also expect that many times you may be on that mountain by yourself or with just a few faithful spiritual warriors.

Although through the cross we now live under grace, understand that there will be a percentage of Christians who will always feel uncomfortable with the concept of waiting on God.

Whether it's due to fear of the unknown, a distain for long periods of prayer, or just Satan's influence to keep God's people away from prayer, spending time in the presence of the Lord has always been a challenge to draw the masses. Any pastor will tell you that it is much easier to call people to a potluck or Christmas party or a church picnic than it is to a time of prayer, especially if there is fasting involved.

As a word of warning, may I also say that it can become very tempting for leaders, out of frustration, to guilt people into praying. As pastors, it's not wise to use the pulpit as a battering ram to get people to give up their time to seek the Lord, or tell them that if they really loved the Lord, and loved their pastor, that they would be there with the leadership in prayer. While this may work for a period of time, and it might actually get a few more involved, if not led by the Holy Spirit, after a while the people will resent the leadership for forcing this practice on them.

Worse yet, these same people may begin to develop a judgmental attitude toward other congregants who are not participating. In either case, their involvement would be useless, because their attitude is wrong.

As leaders, we are called to challenge, we are called to teach, but most of all, we are called to live our lives as examples and allow the Holy Spirit to do His work in leading His people in ways that we can't.

At one point in Exodus 32, Moses was on Mount Sinai for over 40 days and nights alone with God receiving every instruction that God required to give His people. But, when it came to the people, see what Exodus 32:1-4 has to say:

"When the people saw that Moses was so long in coming down from the mountain, they gathered around Aaron and said, "Come, make us gods who will go before us. As for this fellow Moses who brought us up out of Egypt, we don't know what has happened to him." Aaron answered them, "Take off the gold earrings that your wives, your sons and your daughters are wearing, and bring them to me." So all the people took off their earrings and brought them to Aaron. He took what they handed him and made it into an idol cast in the shape of a calf, fashioning it with a tool. Then they said, "These are your gods, who brought you up out of Egypt."

Like Israel, people are really no different today. Because of their lack of understanding of what God desires and requires from us, there will always be those who feel hesitant to seek after the Lord. There will even be times when there are those under your leadership who will feel that they are more in tune with God's will than you are, and will believe that going up the mountain is completely unnecessary and a waste of time.

When you go to the mountaintop and seek after the Lord, don't be surprised when even your peers, your fellow leaders, fail you here. Moses' own brother, Aaron, who stood with him before Pharaoh, who should have known better, became influenced by the whining and complaining of his fellow Israelites while Moses was on the mountain receiving the commandments of the Lord. Rather than supporting his own brother, rather than taking on his role as a spiritual leader amongst the people and encouraging them to support Moses, Aaron allowed them to build the golden calf and even guided them on how to build it!

Even Jesus himself, on the night before His own crucifixion, asked His faithful disciples to watch and pray for just one hour, Yet even in this, they failed and fell asleep and even denied Him the same night.

I would like to remind you again and encourage you, that as I said earlier, learn early in your calling to "hold onto God tightly and people loosely." People will let you down, even those who you would consider your peers. The sooner you understand this reality, the less shocked you will be if and when it happens.

As the called, it is sometimes lonely at the mountaintop because not everyone wants to go there. But, go there you must. Without it, your ministry will remain in the valley where your vision will be limited and be led by the flesh.

In Matthew 17, Jesus climbs to the top of a mountain where he is physically transformed right before the disciples' very eyes. In verses 2-3, we read that Jesus was, "...transfigured before them. His face shone like the sun, and his clothes became as white as the light. Just then there appeared before them Moses and Elijah, talking with Jesus."

Why was it that only Peter, James and John climbed the mountain with Jesus? Where were the other disciples? I personally believe that, just like with Moses on Mt. Sinai, to go with Jesus up that mountain took commitment. To them, it was much easier to stay at the base of the mountain and cheer Jesus on than to climb with Him. The problem is that because the nine disciples chose to stay at the base of the mountain, when it came to spiritual power, those disciples had none.

In verses 14-15, we find out that while Jesus, Peter, James and John were up on the mountain hearing the voice of God the Father, the rest of the disciples were at the base of the mountain dealing with an uncooperative demon! When Jesus came down from the mountain, the boy's father says to Jesus, "I brought him to your disciples, but they could not heal him." What disciples you ask? The ones that did not climb up the mountain with Jesus. They ministered in the flesh and the flesh failed them.

As the called of God, always commit yourself to get away with the Lord, to be refilled with the anointing, refilled with the power of the Holy Spirit, even when no one wants to go with you. If you don't, your strength and authority will quickly weaken and fade. You will be left with trying to build God's spiritual kingdom in the flesh.

When Moses came off of Mt. Sinai, the people could see that he had been with God. Exodus 34:29 says, "When Moses came down from Mount Sinai with the two tablets of the covenant law in his hands, he was not aware that his face was radiant because he had spoken with the Lord."

When the called spend time with the Lord, they become anointed and a powerhouse for God's work. Your calling becomes renewed, your spiritual giftings are refreshed and your followers will sense the reality that you are, indeed, a messenger of the Lord.

Go deep with God, even if you have to go alone. If you do, I promise you, you will continually dwell with the anointing of the Lord.

BELIEVE IN THE PEOPLE THAT FOLLOW YOU

I'm sure most of us have heard someone who has a high tolerance for difficult people described as having the "patience of Job." We know that Job had friends in his life who challenged his patience. But when it came to Moses and patience, now there was a man who had incredible self-control when dealing with complaining people.

As I mentioned earlier, one of my favorite singer/songwriters who influenced my spiritual journey as a young man was Keith Green. One humorous song on his album of the same name that he wrote was called, "So You Wanna Go Back to Egypt." In this song, Keith goes through the story of

Moses and the how the Israelites complained about everything! The song goes on to say that one thing that they were sick of eating most of all was manna. They had "manna bagels; manna waffles; manna burgers and the most famous of all, ba-manna bread." Such as funny song, and so creatively done, that I remember the words to this very day.

Well, Israel sure knew how to find something wrong with absolutely every situation. In such a corrosive environment, it took a special kind of leader to oversee these very "special" people. In fact, Numbers 12:3 says, "Moses was a very humble man, more humble than anyone else on the face of the earth." He had an incredible way of not only leading these people, but also having a tolerance and patience that I challenge you to find in anyone else outside of Jesus himself.

Moses seemed to understand that despite what you do for people, at some point, those same people will let you down. And let him down they did, over and over and over again.

As I wrote in Chapter 5, putting our faith in people, hoping that they will somehow bless us for all our hard work, will inevitably lead to confusion and frustration. As with Moses, I would call that the understatement of the year!

Despite all of his humility, Moses still had his limits. We find one such moment in Numbers 11:11-15a, where after the Israelites demand that Moses provide them with meat to eat, he breaks down and just has it out with God.

"Why have you brought this trouble on your servant? What have I done to displease you that you put the burden of all these people on me? Did I conceive all these people? Did I give them birth? Why do you tell me to carry them in my arms, as a nurse carries an infant, to the land you promised on oath to their ancestors? Where can I get meat for all these people? They keep wailing to me, 'Give us meat to eat!' I cannot carry all these people by myself; the burden is too heavy for me. If this is how you are going to treat me, please go ahead and kill me!"

I could see some in ministry being tempted to have that Scripture printed on the back of their business card!

In early 2018, when I was in Florida at a JMT (John Maxwell Team) Conference, John jokingly mentioned that there was a book that he was writing that would not be published until after he passed away. He said, "If you are in a book store some time and you see this book, say a little prayer for my family, because you will know that I have met my demise. The book would be called, "Leadership Sucks!" (Things that I always wanted to say about leadership while I was alive, but couldn't)."

I love that man's style of humor and honesty! There is no getting around it. When you are in leadership, there will always be people that you lead that can be really mean. They can be praising you one moment and condemning you the next. When you look at Moses, it's hard to imagine how anyone could be so cruel to him after he did so much to deliver these people from 400 years of bondage.

Like most of us, Moses too, had his moments of doubt and frustration. Yet at the end of the day, Moses just kept on leading, kept on serving and kept on loving these people, because that is just what good leaders do.

Young Anne Frank was a girl who kept a diary of her life while hiding from the Nazi's during World War 2. Eventually, her entire family was caught and while in confinement, Anne died with her sister in a concentration camp. After the war, her surviving father discovered her writings, now translated from the original Dutch to over 60 languages. Despite the trauma that she and her family went through, in her journal she wrote the following statement: "In spite of everything, I still believe that people are really good at heart."

To believe in people does not mean that we are naive and gullible. To believe in people does not mean that we don't believe in the depravity of the human heart either. What it does mean is that a strong leader, like Jesus Himself did, believes in people even when they don't believe in themselves.

At the heart of the matter, these people that Moses oversaw, really did not believe in the miracle that God had in store for them.

In Deuteronomy 6:10-12, Moses is describing God's laws and promises to Israel. If they are true to the Lord, then, all His promises are what will be in store for them.

"When the Lord your God brings you into the land he swore to your fathers, to Abraham, Isaac and Jacob, to give you—a land with large, flourishing cities you did not build, houses filled with all kinds of good things you did not provide, wells you did not dig, and vineyards and olive groves you did not plant—then when you eat and are satisfied, be careful that you do not forget the Lord, who brought you out of Egypt, out of the land of slavery."

These were the amazing promises for God's people, if they would just believe. The problem was that this generation did not think like a nation, they thought like slaves. Slavery was all they knew. Despite what awaited them, this generation of Israelites could not comprehend it.

They had been slaves for all their lives and you see this thinking continue in the following event. Not long after they left Egypt, Israel finds themselves standing at the border of the Promised Land of Canaan. Twelve spies were sent out for 40 days to check things out and see what they were up against. They report the following:

"We went into the land to which you sent us, and it does flow with milk and honey! Here is its fruit. But the people who live there are powerful, and the cities are fortified and very large. We even saw descendants of Anak there. The Amalekites live in the Negev; the Hittites, Jebusites and Amorites live in the hill country; and the Canaanites live near the sea and along the Jordan." Then Caleb silenced the people before Moses and said, "We should go up and take possession of the land, for we can certainly do it." But the men who had gone up with him said, "We can't attack those people; they are stronger than we are." And they spread among the Israelites a bad report about the land they had explored" (Numbers 13:27-32a).

Because of who these people were, despite Moses just promising that God was going to give them this land as their inheritance, they could not comprehend that they possessed any power or divine authority to take it over.

The reality is that it's one thing to be given the promise, it's another thing to get your hands dirty to make the promise a reality.

Once the bad report was given by the unbelieving spies, the rumors and gossip began to spread like wildfire throughout the camp.

We read in Numbers 14:1-4, "That night all the members of the community raised their voices and wept aloud. All the Israelites grumbled against Moses and Aaron, and the whole assembly said to them, "If only we had died in Egypt! Or in this wilderness! Why is the Lord bringing us to this land only to let us fall by the sword? Our wives and children will be taken as plunder. Wouldn't it be better for us to go back to Egypt?" And they said to each other, "We should choose a leader and go back to Egypt."

It got so bad, that in verse 10 it says that they hated Moses' leadership so much that they talked about stoning him and his companions.

Now, what would you do as God's leader at this moment? Would you call down fire from heaven to wipe out this ungodly and unruly lot? In the following verses we see God's incredible response to their rebellion, for the Lord says to Moses in verses 11-12, "How long will these people treat me with contempt? How long will they refuse to believe in me, in spite of all the signs I have performed among them? I will strike them down with a plague and destroy them, but I will make you into a nation greater and stronger than they."

God is about to destroy them. But look and see what suddenly happens. Rather than giving God the thumbs up to do away with them, Moses says to the Lord in versus 13b-18:

"...the Egyptians will hear about it! By your power you brought these people up from among them. And they will tell the inhabitants of this land about it. They have already heard that you, Lord, are with these people and that you, Lord, have been seen face to face, that your cloud stays over them, and that you go before them in a pillar of cloud by day and a pillar of fire by night. If you put all these people to death, leaving none alive, the nations who have heard this report about you will say, 'The Lord was not able to bring these people into the land he promised them on oath, so he slaughtered them in the wilderness.' "Now may the Lord's strength be displayed, just as you have declared: 'The Lord is slow to anger, abounding in love and forgiving sin and rebellion. Yet he does not leave the guilty unpunished; he punishes the children for the sin of the parents to the third and fourth generation.'"

Do you see the heart of this leader, Moses?! When God is about to destroy the very ones who wanted Moses stoned, what does he do? Moses stands before the Lord on behalf of the people and pleads for clemency!

As leaders, the test is not how you react when everyone is singing your praises and telling you how anointed you are. The true test of your authenticity will be when everyone seems to be against you. Will your flesh rise up and pray for fire to come down from heaven like James and John wanted, or will you plead to the Lord for mercy and patience?

All through Israel's incredible rebellion and depravity, Moses was still able to believe in their potential and see the bigger picture.

I believe that at that moment, God was giving Moses his first real test after his Mt. Sinai experience. God knew who Moses was dealing with when it came to these people, but the question was, was Moses ready? Was he willing to put up with all their garbage for the next 40 years?

This trip through the wilderness should have finished there. These people, after seeing all of God's miracles and his authority on Mt. Sinai, should have believed in the good reports of the Promised Land and moved forward into their destiny. But they refused to believe and they feared their enemies.

At that moment, Moses was exposed to what kind of people he would be dealing with for the rest of his life. Was he ready for that? Was he willing to surrender everything to lead a people who seemed to show no appreciation, no respect for his authority?

One question you might be thinking is, "Was God actually going to destroy them?" Maybe. But more importantly, God was allowing Moses to be tested to see for himself if he was willing to continue on this difficult journey.

When we are called to lead, we are called to believe in those who follow us. No matter what they say or don't say, no matter what they do or don't do. We must believe in them more than they believe in themselves. They, like this first generation of Israelites, may never see their blessings fulfilled. They may never get to their Promised Land because of their rebellion and unbelief, but that is God's call, not yours.

I have witnessed ministry leaders speaking curses on the people they oversee. Because of their own frustrations, these leaders have spoken death on fellow Christians rather than life.

There are always times for rebuking, times for chastisement and discipline. In fact, that is part of our calling. Yet even in the most difficult of situations, as servants of the Lord, we are called to always deal with difficulties such as these, coated in love and with the highest respect for those we serve (I Corinthians 16:14).

The church at Corinth was Paul's biggest nightmare when it came to dysfunctional behavior. This assembly of believers were so messed up that he had to deal with issues of incest, adultery, idolatry, you name it - it was in the church! Yet overall, Paul loved this group of believers. Look at how he addresses them before dealing with their sinful behavior. In 1 Corinthians 1:1-6 (emphasis added), he says the following:

"Paul, called to be an apostle of Christ Jesus by the will of God, and our brother Sosthenes, To the church of God in Corinth, to those sanctified

<u>in Christ Jesus and called to be his holy people,</u> together with all those everywhere who call on the name of our Lord Jesus Christ—their Lord and ours: <u>Grace and peace to you from God our Father and the Lord Jesus Christ. I always thank my God for you because of his grace given you in Christ Jesus.</u> For in him you have been enriched in every way—with all kinds of speech and with all knowledge— <u>God thus confirming our testimony about Christ among you."</u>

Isn't that amazing? Notice what I've underlined above. Paul was not overlooking their sins, not making excuses for their bad behavior, but looking at sin for what it is, calling it out, dealing with the rebellion and believing for a good outcome. Paul is actually reminding them who they are in Christ and thereby challenging them in a loving way to raise their standards.

Moses would be dealing with continual rebellion from this generation of Israelites for the rest of his life. Yet something tells me that they weren't the ones he kept his focus on. For amongst those thousands upon thousands of people, Moses had his Calebs, he had his Aarons, his Hurs, his Joshuas. These and many more were his faithful followers who, although not perfect, believed in their leader and continued to support him.

As the called, you will always have those who take more than they give. There will be those who drain you more than fill you. But don't let these individuals dictate who you are as a leader. Love everybody – yet knowing that sometimes there are those who are best loved from a distance.

I love the quote from Mahatma Gandhi, which says, "I will not let anyone walk through my mind with their dirty feet." As leaders, we must lead every person that God has placed us over, but don't let the pollution of these carnal, negative, visionless individuals distort your view of yourself or what God desires to do through you, his called!

LEARN TO DELEGATE

When God is using us in ministry, there is a danger to hold onto our vision and our passion like a precious newborn baby. For many in ministry, it can become difficult to take that vision and try to pass it onto others to help us fulfill that dream out of fear that the dream might become mismanaged.

Micromanaging is the proverbial Achilles heel when it comes to visionaries, which many called people are. They see the vision, they have a clear sense that this is the will of God, believing that with just a little hard work, their vision will quickly become a reality. Unfortunately, many called visionaries become frustrated and disillusioned when their many hours of endless sweat and tears seemingly go unappreciated by those looking on, and perhaps cheering on. In the end, the vision remains just that, a vision. The problem wasn't the vision, the problem was that they failed to create the team around them who would catch the vision and run with it.

There is a quote from John Maxwell regarding delegation that I need to share from his book, <u>Becoming a Person of Influence</u>. It's a bit long, but it's too good just to share only a part of it.

"The ability to empower others is one of the keys to personal and professional success. John Craig remarked, "No matter how much work you can do, no matter how engaging your personality may be, you will not advance far in business if you cannot work through others." And business executive J. Paul Getty asserted, "It doesn't make much difference how much other knowledge or experience an executive possesses; if he is unable to achieve results through people, he is worthless as an executive."

"When you become an empowerer, you work with and through people, but you do much more. You enable others to reach the highest levels in their personal and professional development. Simply defined, empowering is giving your influence to others for the purpose of personal and organizational growth. It's sharing yourself – your influence, position, power and opportunities – with others with the purpose of investing in their lives so that they can function at their best. It's seeing people's potential, sharing your resources with them, and showing them that you believe in them completely.

"The act of empowering others changes lives, and it's a win-win situation for you and the people you empower. Giving others your authority isn't like giving away an object, such as your car. If you give away your car, you're stuck. You no longer have transportation. But empowering others by giving them your authority has the same effect as sharing information: you haven't lost anything. You have increased the ability of others without decreasing yourself."

As shared earlier in Ephesians 4:11, "So Christ himself gave the apostles, the prophets, the evangelists, the pastors and teachers," but as we continue on to verses 12-13a, we see why – "to equip his people for works of service, so that the body of Christ may be built up until we all reach unity in the faith."

According to Paul, as the called, a major part of our calling is to equip His people for works of service. In accomplishing this task, one's vision must not just be shared, but must actually be caught by those you are called to equip.

In Exodus, Chapters 17 and 18, we find two situations that involve Moses and the Israelites that clearly deal with this very aspect of delegation.

After the moment with God providing water from the rock in Rephidim, Israel is then confronted by the Amalekites who are determined to destroy them before they ever make it to the Promised Land. In Exodus 17:10-13, we read:

"So Joshua fought the Amalekites as Moses had ordered, and Moses, Aaron and Hur went to the top of the hill. As long as Moses held up his hands, the Israelites were winning, but whenever he lowered his hands, the Amalekites were winning. When Moses' hands grew tired, they took a stone and put it under him and he sat on it. Aaron and Hur held his hands up—one on one side, one on the other—so that his hands remained steady till sunset. So Joshua overcame the Amalekite army with the sword."

That day Moses learned a very important lesson, which was to share the victory. If Moses had not allowed the support from Aaron and Hur, the outcome of that battle would have been very different. If Moses would have said, "I'm God's leader, I'm fine alone, it's my responsibility to oversee our victory, stand back and observe the victory of the Lord," (I'm typing that in my best Charlton Heston voice), not only would Moses have not experienced the victory, but all of Israel would have been decimated as well.

At the end of the day during the victory party, I am sure there was a lot of talk going on about Aaron's and Hur's role in the battle. Perhaps there were a few jokes flying around the campfires regarding those "arms up – winning, arms down – losing" moments.

It might have been God's instruction for Moses to keep his arms extended, but it was Aaron and Hur that kept them there. And with Joshua leading the battle, it definitely was a team effort that won the victory.

As John Maxwell states in the previous quote, "It's sharing yourself – your influence, position, power and opportunities," that make people come alive and feel excited about the influence that they are also contributing to the team. When that happens, loyalty is refined. People are much more committed and supportive when they feel that they have some skin in the game. Teach them the important role that they have, knowing fully well that they may be the very individuals that you may be passing your mantle to one day.

Going ahead a few verses into Exodus 18:11-12, we find Moses' father-in-law, Jethro, along with Moses' wife and two sons, making an unexpected visit to Moses after hearing all that God was doing through him.

Jethro was extremely impressed with everything that God was doing through his son-in-law, Moses. So much so that he says, ""Now I know that the Lord is greater than all other gods, for He did this to those who had treated

Israel arrogantly." Then Jethro, brought a burnt offering and other sacrifices to God, and Aaron came with all the elders of Israel to eat a meal with Moses' father-in-law in the presence of God."

Jethro is undoubtedly a proud father-in-law. Even with all the accolades and praises bestowed upon Moses, Jethro discovered very quickly that there was room for improvement. In verses 13-16, we read the following:

"The next day Moses took his seat to serve as judge for the people, and they stood around him from morning till evening. When his father-in-law saw all that Moses was doing for the people, he said, "What is this you are doing for the people? Why do you alone sit as judge, while all these people stand around you from morning till evening?" Moses answered him, "Because the people come to me to seek God's will. Whenever they have a dispute, it is brought to me, and I decide between the parties and inform them of God's decrees and instructions."

Now try to imagine with me what is going on here. The Bible says that Moses each day, "took his seat to serve as judge for the people." "What people?" you might ask. How about all the people? How about the million plus people that Israel consisted of? And "all these people stood around him from morning till evening."

As a called person, one thing that you may find yourself doing, from time to time, depending on what type of ministry you are involved in, is personal counseling. Even though you may never receive an official degree in that field, you will find that people will many times be naturally drawn to you for advice because of the mantle of the anointing that you carry. The truth is, while there may be some situations that require your personal involvement and guidance, there are a number of situations that should be passed on to individuals who are much more gifted and certified in dealing with those unique situations.

A called man or woman needs to be cautious of the 'need to be needed' addiction that can unknowingly begin to control your decisions. People will call you saying they just need to talk with you. People will send you emails and messages telling you that no one else understands their situation like you do.

If you are not careful, this can become a very controlling behavior that will quickly overwhelm your entire ministry and make you completely ineffective.

Moses' father-in-law can see right away that Moses has fallen into this same trap. Everyone was in need of Moses' attention. If he had continued to allow them to abuse him this way, it would have destroyed his calling and his mental well-being. Jethro says to Moses in Exodus 18:17-23:

"What you are doing is not good. You and these people who come to you will only wear yourselves out. The work is too heavy for you; you cannot handle it alone. Listen now to me and I will give you some advice, and may God be with you. You must be the people's representative before God and bring their disputes to him. Teach them his decrees and instructions, and show them the way they are to live and how they are to behave. But select capable men from all the people—men who fear God, trustworthy men who hate dishonest gain—and appoint them as officials over thousands, hundreds, fifties and tens. Have them serve as judges for the people at all times, but have them bring every difficult case to you; the simple cases they can decide themselves. That will make your load lighter, because they will share it with you. If you do this and God so commands, you will be able to stand the strain, and all these people will go home satisfied."

Whether it was Aaron and Hur lifting Moses' hands, or finding gifted leaders who were honest and trustworthy who could share in overseeing the peoples' disputes, Moses needed to learn, and learn quickly, to equip God's people for works of service.

To equip and to delegate work to others isn't about giving someone else jobs that we don't want to do. Moses still personally judged the most difficult cases himself. What delegation does is free your time up to use your gifting more effectively, while at the same time training up future leaders to reach their greatest potential.

Moses would have never survived his first year in the wilderness, let alone the next 40, if he didn't learn the art of delegation.

I call it an art because in order to delegate effectively, you have to develop a discerning spirit to know how to use your own time and giftings wisely. At the same time, you need to be committed to building a solid team around you. Those who have the potential, willingness and teachable spirit to take on some of the responsibilities from you will also have the opportunity to develop their own leadership skills.

I can think of several occasions when I made the decision to delegate certain responsibilities to others, yet because they were not the right fit or ill prepared, it caused more frustration, stress and extra work for me than it was worth.

Look for people who are first of all loyal to your leadership. Not that they worship the ground you walk on, but they understand your role, respect you as a leader and have a passion to help fulfill the vision the Lord gave you. When you find these individuals, pour into their lives all you can. Take time each week to give them opportunities of learning and development, while at the same time sharing your vision and hearing their heart.

When you look at the people who were closest to Moses, many young men definitely stood with him, but it was only Joshua who rose to the position of Moses' protégé. In the end, it was Joshua who became the one who would lead the next generation of Israelites into the Promised Land.

Early on in Exodus 17, as Moses is keeping records of Israel's accomplishments and victories over their enemies, the Lord says to Moses in verse 14, "Write this on a scroll as something to be remembered and make sure that Joshua hears it, because I will completely blot out the name of Amalek from under heaven."

With Joshua by Moses' side, God was assuring that Israel would continue having a capable leader even long after Moses had passed.

The Calling of Moses

We see Joshua close by Moses again in Exodus 24:12-13, "The Lord said to Moses, "Come up to me on the mountain and stay here, and I will give you the tablets of stone with the law and commandments I have written for their instruction." Then Moses set out with Joshua, his aide, and Moses went up on the mountain of God."

When the tabernacle was established for worship, and the presence of the Lord descended upon it in the form of a cloud, we read in Exodus 33:10-11, "Whenever the people saw the pillar of cloud standing at the entrance to the tent, they all stood and worshiped, each at the entrance to their tent. The Lord would speak to Moses face to face, as one speaks to a friend. Then Moses would return to the camp, but his young aide Joshua son of Nun did not leave the tent."

Joshua obviously had his own personal experience with the Lord. When Moses left the tent after his duties were complete, Joshua stayed there, continuously soaking in the presence of the Lord. I have discovered that when you have good mentees around you, not only will you be pouring into their lives, but they will feed your soul as well, and Joshua did this very well with Moses.

In the end, after 40 years of wandering in the wilderness, Moses was not permitted to cross over into the land of Canaan. Because of his disobedience in the desert of Zin, where he struck the rock twice instead of speaking to it, God disallowed Moses to lead any further and was called to pass his mantle to Joshua. In Numbers 27:18-20, just before Moses is about to die, we read, "So the Lord said to Moses, "Take Joshua son of Nun, a man in whom is the spirit of leadership, and lay your hand on him. Have him stand before Eleazar the priest and the entire assembly and commission him in their presence. Give him some of your authority so the whole Israelite community will obey him."

Whether it is Elijah with Elisha, or Moses with Joshua, the greatest honor that any called individual could ever do is to pass their mantle, their authority, to the next generation.

When we learn to delegate, we do more than just give others the opportunity of sharing the load. We also have the privilege of directing others toward their own calling where, like Elisha, they just might receive a double portion of what God flowed through you.

LEGACY OF MOSES

Moses' legacy is so expansive, so transformative, that it's pretty well impossible to try to get it all down in just a few pages. So, I just want to focus on a couple of very important aspects of Moses' impact. Moses' impact on the world was not just a Jewish thing. Through this leader, God passed down to the world the blueprint of redemption that would eventually lead straight to the cross of Calvary.

Moses is given credit by many reputable scholars and theologians as being the author of the first five books of the Bible, known as the Pentateuch (or the Torah). The Torah, which derives the very meaning and purpose of our world's existence, also displays the genesis of God's redemptive plan to restore sinful man back to himself.

Where Abraham may have birthed the nation of God, it was Moses and the Mosaic laws and commandments that breathed spiritual life into them. This life gave them the moral authority and principles that would change not only them, but also every nation that chose to base their belief system on the Judeo-Christian values.

Moses' character displayed a type of Christ in that he took on the role as mediator, who was willing to lay down his life as he stood between the holiness of God and the sinfulness and rebellion of God's people, Israel. As stated earlier, he believed in them more than they believed in him, having no idea that it was Moses himself that was keeping them from experiencing the full vent of God's wrath.

Paul writes about Jesus being our mediator when he says in 1 Timothy

2:5-6, "For there is one God and one mediator between God and mankind, the man Christ Jesus, who gave himself as a ransom for all people. This has now been witnessed to at the proper time." Also, in Hebrews 9:15, we read, "For this reason Christ is the mediator of a new covenant, that those who are called may receive the promised eternal inheritance."

Jesus stands today through the cross as the mediator in which we are able to cry out, "Abba, Father" and take up our inheritance. In the same way, Moses was the one who enabled God's people to leave their slavery and enter into their rest, into their adoption, as they crossed over the Jordan into the Promised Land (their inheritance).

This comparison is clearly seen when Paul says in Romans 8:15, "The Spirit you received does not make you slaves, so that you live in fear again; rather, the Spirit you received brought about your adoption to sonship. And by him we cry, "Abba, Father."

Where the whole first generation of Israelites, apart from Joshua and Caleb, died in the wilderness, it was their children, the next generation that crossed over once and for all. Unlike their parents, this next generation chose to trust and obey the Mosaic law that God required.

As the called, Moses' legacy should challenge us, that just as he gave Israel the entirety of the law despite many of its difficult guidelines, we also, now under grace, are obligated to present the "full gospel" of Christ. Proclaiming His grace, yet also His holiness. Teaching about His forgiveness, yet never neglecting the reality of a soul being lost outside of the cross. Paul writes in Acts 20:27, "For I have not hesitated to proclaim to you the whole will of God."

Although it might be tempting at times to avoid certain aspects of the gospel message because it might sound too demanding for your listeners, like Paul, there can't be any hesitation or apprehension on our part. Regardless of this politically correct climate we find ourselves living amongst in North America, presenting only the part of the Bible that the world finds palatable is not only incomplete, it's actually dangerous and irresponsible. This makes the good news of the gospel message no message at all.

As the called, we can never allow ourselves to be representers of only a sweet little baby Jesus kind of gospel; a message that presents all the niceties and no meat! Although this pablum kind of gospel can be tempting to give, scratching where people may feel they have an itch, it serves no purpose in helping the lost confront the issue of sin and find salvation through Jesus.

I would compare this kind of message to a pain-killer given to a person that is dying. You convince them that because the pain is no longer there, that they are healed. Yet, unknown to them, on the inside the disease continues to destroy them.

We are responsible to present the entire message. All the way to the cruel, ugly cross with all it's blood and gore because "without the shedding of blood there is not forgiveness of sin" (Hebrews 9:22).

When Moses came off of Mt. Sinai, he had the difficult task of presenting to the people all the rules and regulations of how to live, worship and thrive as a nation. He had to teach them that they were, indeed, sinners and in desperate need of God's intervention.

The guidelines were difficult, they were intense, and they were detailed. Yet nowhere do we see Moses hesitating to teach the people what God commanded them to do. He presented it all. And although he was met with much resistance, he remained steadfast and disciplined in what was required of him.

Moses not only presented what God gave him for the people, he also lived it out himself. Everything that he commanded of the Israelites, he himself was willing to follow. As the called, in the same way, you are required by the Lord to live such an exemplary, disciplined life of godliness that people will most naturally want to believe and trust in God, because they believe and trust in you.

The next generation of Israelites believed and trusted in Joshua, because Joshua believed and trusted in his mentor, Moses. As leaders, if we are not raising up future men and women of God to seek after and commit themselves to their calling, then we have failed in what I believe is our most important task of all.

The older I get, the more I realize that there are some tasks in Christian leadership that are much more suited to a younger generation. Where I once was part of that young group of dare-devil servants of God, I now have discovered that as the years have ticked by, my role has evolved into helping a new generation of young called men and women to understand and grasp the full potential of their own calling. This is one reason why I wrote this book.

For a man who lived over 3,200 years ago, whose name is mentioned over 750 times in the Older Testament and over 80 times in the Newer Testament, Moses obviously made a huge impact.

One of the largest impacts I would say is that he believed in people. He believed that people had value and were worth pouring time into. Whether it was saving the life of the slave being beaten in Egypt, leading, teaching and overseeing the nation of Israel, or spending hours mentoring his protégé, Joshua. Moses believed the best of people and that is why God trusted Moses to lead His people in the first place.

I have discovered over the years, that people remember very few of my sermons, or the depth of my understanding of God's Word. What they remember is if I cared for them or not. Did I inspire them to believe in a God who believes in them? Did I motivate them to dig deeper in their passion for the Lord, because they saw that same passion in my life? How did I make them feel? Did I belittle them or did I stir within them a curiosity to want to know Jesus better? Once again, "People don't care how much you know until they know how much you care."

That was Moses. That was his legacy. He loved people no matter what circumstances he found himself in, and over three millennials later, we are still inspired by him!

CHAPTER 7

THE CALLING OF DAVID

LINEAGE OF DAVID

Out of all the Older Testament Patriarchs, King David is arguably one that is the most well-known and spoken about, not only for his own accolades and accomplishments during his reign, but also regarding future prophetic events that will involve David's throne, including when Jesus himself will sit on David's throne during the future millennial kingdom (Psalm 132:11-12; Isaiah 9:7; Luke 1:32-33).

It is even believed in Jewish tradition that King David himself will be resurrected to reign on his throne with the Messiah during this incredible future event.

This is quite impressive, considering that even David's father, Jesse, felt there was nothing in David that even came close to resembling the makings of a king.

The Bible says that David's family were herdsmen. But there is much more to this family than meets the eye. Go back just a couple of generations and you discover that David's father was the son of Ohed, who was the son of Boaz and Ruth.

The story of Boaz and Ruth is a wonderful love story of a man who was willing to redeem a widowed girl who wasn't even Jewish. Out of her love for her mother-in-law, Naomi, Ruth chose to move to the Promised Land and assimilate into the Jewish culture and their worship of the God of Israel.

It is from this family line that the gospel of Matthew, Chapter 1 reminds us of God's ultimate plan.

Matthew goes through great detail in giving the lineage of Jesus. Starting with Abraham, he makes reference to over forty-two generations, mentioning Boaz, Ruth, Ohed, Jesse, David and so on, until he finally comes to Jesus himself.

The family of Jesse was chosen because of God's future plan of salvation through Jesse's descendants. David was chosen from all his other brothers because of what God saw in young David himself.

HUMILITY

In 1 Samuel 15:4-5, the Bible says, "Samuel did what the Lord said. When he arrived at Bethlehem, the elders of the town trembled when they met him. They asked, "Do you come in peace?" Samuel replied, "Yes, in peace; I have come to sacrifice to the Lord. Consecrate yourselves and come to the sacrifice with me." Then he consecrated Jesse and his sons and invited them to the sacrifice."

In this chapter, the Lord commands the prophet Samuel to go to the town of Bethlehem to anoint the next King of Israel, as He had forsaken Saul because of his rebellious spirit.

Now, let's look to see what is happening here. We just read that the word was going around town that Samuel, the prophet of God, was coming to town. It was such a big event that verse four tells us that the elders of Bethlehem came to greet him, including Jesse and his sons; all of them except, of course, young David.

The Calling of David

While all of the hype of Samuel's visit was taking place, where was David? He was doing what he was called to do, taking care of his father's sheep.

David quite likely knew of the prophet's unexpected visit. Everyone was talking about it. After all, it's not everyday that the messenger of the Lord comes to your small community. Yet, David was nowhere near all this fanfair. He was humbly doing what his father asked him to do. The future shepherd of God's people, Israel, was learning his trade amongst the sheep. After all, wasn't it amongst the sheep where David protected them by killing the bear and lion? Wasn't it amongst the sheep where David learned how to perfect the use of the sling that would eventually kill Goliath?

The humble servant of the Lord understands this. They never "despise the day of small beginnings," because they understand that it is these everyday experiences that are the learning grounds to greater challenges down the road (Zechariah 4:10).

Because humility is the vital and essential foundation of any called individual, sooner or later the one who is called will have to experience the challenges that help develop this all too important attribute in their character.

For some who begin life with an over-indulgence of self-confidence, humility will need to be marinated within them over and over again until any scent of their pompous, self-centered, self-righteousness is finally dissolved away.

What was it that David had that God could see which his older brothers did not possess? I believe it was his humble faith that was slowly being developed within him while out taking care of Jesse's flock.

Nobody knew it was happening, perhaps not even young David himself. Yet when Samuel went through all David's brothers one by one, it was only David, who was nowhere to be seen, that God knew was the chosen one.

If you would compare the two young men of David to Joseph, you would see that this time of their lives as young boys is strikingly different. Where

Joseph saw himself as a leader early on in life, even telling his bothers of the dreams that God was giving him about the day when he would rule over them, David was nothing like this.

Where Joseph had to be brought down a few notches in his preparation for his calling, David, in actuality, had to be brought up and trained by the Holy Spirit himself while out amongst the sheep.

In 1 Samuel 16:10-12, it says, "Jesse had seven of his sons pass before Samuel, but Samuel said to him, "The Lord has not chosen these." So he asked Jesse, "Are these all the sons you have?" "There is still the youngest," Jesse answered. "He is tending the sheep." Samuel said, "Send for him; we will not sit down until he arrives." So he sent for him and had him brought in. He was glowing with health and had a fine appearance and handsome features. Then the Lord said, "Rise and anoint him; this is the one."

When it comes to the calling, it is unfortunate that many young men and women visualize being in the spotlight of working for the Lord more than anything else. Somewhere, they missed the paralleled comparison of living the character of Jesus who said that he "came not to be served but to serve and give his life as a ransom for many" (Matthew 20:28).

Jesus again deals with this issue in Luke 14:7-11, where we read that while he was at a guest's home:

"He noticed how the guests picked the places of honor at the table, (and in response to this) he told them this parable: "When someone invites you to a wedding feast, do not take the place of honor, for a person more distinguished than you may have been invited. If so, the host who invited both of you will come and say to you, 'Give this person your seat.' Then, humiliated, you will have to take the least important place. But when you are invited, take the lowest place, so that when your host comes, he will say to you, 'Friend, move up to a better place.' Then you will be honored in the presence of all the other guests. For all those who exalt themselves will be humbled, and those who humble themselves will be exalted."

The Calling of David

I remember working with a young pastor who had just moved from another country. Early on in his ministry with me, he had a difficult time understanding why I, the lead pastor, would involve myself in doing everyday activities at the church. One Sunday morning, we were getting ready to load up my truck with church supplies for our annual church picnic. Looking at me wild-eyed, he said, "Pastor, you would never see that in my country! Pastors never do any physical labor for the church, that's for the lay people!"

Another time, I was preaching in Africa and before the crusade, we were sitting in a room waiting for the service to start. One of the main pastors, who was a bit too oversized for his own good, motioned to one of his understudies to come over and tie his shoes, because he was too overweight to tie them himself.

Without any hesitation, this young man quickly sprinted across the room to take care of his pastor's shoelaces. The pastor just sat back in his chair and showed no appreciation toward this young man for helping him out. I've got to be honest with you, all I could think at that moment was, if that was me, I probably would have tied his shoelaces together to teach that pastor a lesson on humility.

Something tells me that this pastor's behavior was not exactly what took place at the Last Supper. It was Jesus who was doing the kneeling at the feet of the disciples. Of course, Jesus being their leader, even Peter had a hard time in allowing Jesus to do such a lowly task and said to him, "You shall never wash my feet." In response, Jesus said something that every called person needs to take to heart, "Unless I wash you, you have no part with me" (John 13:8).

The illustration that Jesus was teaching His disciples was one that the disciples needed to learn if they were ever to become the leaders that Jesus was preparing them to be. In saying, "you will have no part with me," Jesus was stressing that you will never be a part of the called, unless you are willing to humbly serve others.

Many potential called individuals prefer to see the Peter preaching to thousand, but fail to visit the Peter suffering in prison. They visualize the Paul proclaiming the gospel before Felix in Caesarea in Acts 24, but forget the blind Paul being led by the hand of Ananias in Acts 9.

Sooner or later, the called man or woman has to deal with the issue of pride.

For Joseph, he was forced to come to grips with it when sold into slavery and wrongly imprisoned. David, on the other hand, had to confront it later on in his life. Where humility was a huge part of the reason he was chosen as king in the first place, it was only a number of years later that things all changed and pride got the best of him.

It is in 2 Samuel 11 that we find this same young man having to be confronted by the prophet Nathan after committing adultery and murder. Pride had obviously taken its toll.

Humility is a very difficult characteristic to hold on to. For as soon as you think you have it, it proves that at that very moment of thinking such a self-righteous thought, you are beginning to loose it.

Pride, on the other hand, is like an unruly, untamed monkey, trying every opportunity it can to leap on your back and control your actions. As soon as a moment of success comes your way, as soon as you get that first commendation or praise from others for being used by God, pride is there to scratch that needed itch. It will fill your mind with self-righteousness.

The truth is, pride is no laughing matter. The Bible says in James 4:6 that, "God opposes the proud but shows favor to the humble." Therefore, when pride begins to make its home in the heart of the anointed, the results can be devastating. As leaders, I think the last thing we should ever want is God opposing us; resisting our ministry and working against our goals! Yet that is exactly what can happen to the leader who begins to develop pride.

I have witnessed leaders and lay people alike who God had used in the gifts of the Spirit, yet as time went on, these same people began to identify themselves as no longer a servant of the Lord, but rather one who had a "gift from the Lord."

There is a difference; a big difference between the two and the one who refuses to understand this is bound for a shocking reality check.

When you read the stories of Daniel and Joseph, both of these men realized that their gifts of interpreting dreams had nothing to do with their ability, but rather God speaking through them.

When King Nebuchadnezzar heard that Daniel could interpret dreams, he asks him in Daniel 2:26, "Are you able to tell me what I saw in my dream and interpret it?" Now listen to Daniel's response in verses 27-28: " Daniel replied, "No wise man, enchanter, magician or diviner can explain to the king the mystery he has asked about, but there is a God in heaven who reveals mysteries. He has shown King Nebuchadnezzar what will happen in days to come."

"Did you catch that? He said basically, "Nope, not me – I can't do it, "but there is a God in heaven who reveals mysteries."

No matter what you discover your ministerial giftings are, always remember that it is only God working through you, and you are just the vessel.

In 2007, I came home from an African missions trip to discover that when I stepped off the plane, I lost the majority of my hearing in my right ear. After a few months with no change, the doctor finally concluded that my hearing loss was permanent. It turned out that the medication that I took to prevent malaria while in Africa actually was the cause of the damage.

I'll be honest with you, I was devastated. I thought, "how could I ever continue to be a pastor when I can't even hear people?" The fear was real, and for a period of time, I began to wonder if I could even continue in ministry.

Well, with the technology of hearing aides and the prayers of many, I have managed to live, and yes, minister with my disability.

Through it all, one thing that I learned was that everything I am is because He has enabled it. It should never be taken for granted and the truth is that you are only where you are because God allows it. Everything could be lost in an instant, therefore, we must always acknowledge that our giftings are exactly that, a "gift." Just like Nebuchadnezzar's kingdom, it can be taken in an instant. The prideful don't understand this and the humble are continually aware of this. Looking back now after all these years, I have to say that losing my hearing changed me. It reminded me that everything that I am, everything that I do, I do it because for the moment He has allowed me to.

In David's youth, he understood this. When he shouted out to Goliath, "You come against me with sword and spear and javelin, but I come against you in the name of the Lord Almighty, the God of the armies of Israel, whom you have defied (1 Samuel 17:45), he understood where his strength came from. He was fully aware of who he was up against, and he understood who it was that was going to bring this giant down, and it wasn't David. It was the God of Israel Himself.

That is humility and that is what will sustain you no matter what victories or challenges face you in the roads ahead.

SELF RELIANCE

When we think of someone who is self-reliant, we many times think of someone who has self-confidence. No doubt this is true for anyone who has become successful in life and has made something from nothing.

These people have the wherewithal to focus on their ultimate plans and goals, despite opposing opinions and viewpoints and do what needs to be done.

The called individual is also a man or woman who would fit this description. Yet to the one who is called, they have learned over time that their self-reliance was not based upon themselves alone, but rather on the presence of God who lives in them.

Where the world would initially believe that this person's self-reliance is an inner confidence in themself, once one got to know the values that this called person lives by, they would quickly discover that this self-reliance is, in actuality, a God-reliance. They are able to step out in faith into the seemingly dangerous and impossible situations because of their reliance on the Lord.

From a young age, David was a man who had this self-reliance. His sense of confidence, as I mentioned earlier, was nurtured and developed in moments of insurmountable odds that were stacked against him.

Standing over the dead bear or lion that he killed as a child gave him great stories to tell his family. But it also birthed within him the understanding that there was a God who was not only protecting him, but also calling him to something bigger.

We can notice this when the prophet Samuel anoints him as King in 1 Samuel 16:12-13, "So he sent for him and had him brought in. He was glowing with health and had a fine appearance and handsome features. Then the Lord said, "Rise and anoint him; this is the one." So Samuel took the horn of oil and anointed him in the presence of his brothers, and from that day on the Spirit of the Lord came powerfully upon David."

Unlike King Saul before him, nowhere do we read in these verses David opposing or resisting the mantle that Samuel was placing upon him. He bowed his head, allowed the horn of oil to be poured over him and from that point on it says "the Spirit of the Lord came powerfully upon David."

Compare this to David's predecessor, King Saul, and you will see a stark difference. In 1 Samuel 10:20-24, when the prophet Samuel presents King Saul to Israel, we see:

"When Samuel had all Israel come forward by tribes, the tribe of Benjamin was taken by lot. Then he brought forward the tribe of Benjamin, clan by clan, and Matri's clan was taken. Finally Saul son of Kish was taken. But when they looked for him, he was not to be found. So they inquired further of the Lord,

"Has the man come here yet?" And the Lord said, "Yes, he has hidden himself among the supplies." They ran and brought him out, and as he stood among the people he was a head taller than any of the others. Samuel said to all the people, "Do you see the man the Lord has chosen? There is no one like him among all the people." Then the people shouted, "Long live the king!"

Now forgive me for using this comparison, but when I read this story, it comes across to me almost like some kind of Monty Python comic routine. Imagine this with me. Here is Samuel standing before all of Israel, and after going from clan to clan, family to family, he comes right down to Saul.

As he is about to proclaim, "Behold your King," Saul is nowhere to be found! And where is he? The Lord revealed to Samuel that, "He was hiding among the supplies." Not exactly a great start for Israel's first monarchy.

Throughout his reign, King Saul never really felt confident in his divine calling as King. He hungered for the praise of men and because he didn't have the self-reliance to believe in the position that God put him in, he was always willing to compromise his convictions.

When he began to hear the chants that "Saul killed his thousands, but David killed his tens of thousands," Saul was unable to handle this rejection. As jealousy and bitterness began to fill his heart, his anointing and calling began to dissipate.

This is something that you don't see in young David. Even when Saul was out to kill him, and David was forced to live in the wilderness away from his family, David's self-reliance and belief in his calling sustained him to keep on going. In fact some of the most anointed, heavenly inspired Psalms that we have in our Bible were written by David when he was in that wilderness experience.

In 1 Samuel 24:5-7, when he had the opportunity to kill Saul in the cave of En Gedi, David chose not to, despite his men encouraging him to do so. Instead, David crawled up to Saul and cut off the corner of his robe to show

Saul that David could have killed him if he had wanted to. Yet even with that gesture, even with all his self-control in fighting the flesh, we read:

"Afterward, David was conscience-stricken for having cut off a corner of his robe. He said to his men, "The Lord forbid that I should do such a thing to my master, the Lord's anointed, or lay my hand on him; for he is the anointed of the Lord." With these words David sharply rebuked his men and did not allow them to attack Saul. And Saul left the cave and went his way."

Who has that type of self-control and conviction? The answer is, the called man or woman who has a self-reliance based on their faith in God. They don't have to take matters into their own hands in order to help God along in their calling, because they trust that the Lord will establish them in the proper time.

To be called by God requires a man or woman to be so self-reliant in their faith in the Lord, that despite the oppositions, despite the pressure to give into the flesh and be led by one's feelings, the called of God know the difference between God's timing and their own emotional desires.

Like Joseph, David didn't need the accolades of his brothers to know who he was. When David's brothers, along with the whole army of Israel, were cowering with King Saul over fear of the strength of Goliath, what was David's response to their enemy?

"David said to the Philistine, "You come against me with sword and spear and javelin, but I come against you in the name of the Lord Almighty, the God of the armies of Israel, whom you have defied" (1 Samuel 17:45).

The training that young David received while faithfully and quietly guarding his father's sheep was now fully revealed to all. With the deep thud of Goliath's lifeless body tumbling to the ground, David's life would never be the same and he would forever be known as the giant killer.

God is looking for leaders with that same passion, that same enthusiasm and hunger within their souls, where they will do the right thing. Not necessarily because it is popular, or acceptable or politically correct, but rather because it is God's will. They are unafraid of the opposition that they may receive because of their choices.

Self-reliance is what Jesus was expressing in Matthew 12:48-50, when while teaching he was told that His mother and brothers were waiting to talk with Him outside. In response, He said, "Who is my mother, and who are my brothers?" Pointing to his disciples, he said, "Here are my mother and my brothers. For whoever does the will of my Father in heaven is my brother and sister and mother."

Jesus wasn't denying the existence of His family or suggesting that they held no importance to Him, but what He was trying to bring across was what He made very clear in Luke 14:26, "If anyone comes to me and does not hate their father and mother, wife and children, brothers and sisters—yes, even their own life—such a person cannot be my disciple."

The Apostle Paul also mentions this seemingly irrational concept in 1 Corinthians 7:29-31, when he encourages his readers, saying, "What I mean, brothers and sisters, is that the time is short. From now on those who have wives should live as if they do not; those who mourn, as if they did not; those who are happy, as if they were not; those who buy something, as if it were not theirs to keep; those who use the things of the world, as if not engrossed in them. For this world in its present form is passing away."

From the outside, one might be thinking that both Jesus and Paul were suggesting that hating our family and even hating one's own life, or denying that we are even married, is not only acceptable, but encouraged. Yet the truth is, the self-reliance in your calling will bring you to the place where those on the outside looking in, especially those who do not have the spirit of Christ living in them, will look at you as one who is a bit out of touch with reality.

They will see the choices you are making for God and perhaps begin to think and verbalize that you hate your family or even hate yourself for not staying close to home. For why would anyone leave a healthy, loving home environment and live a life that in their mind is filled with loneliness,

The Calling of David

separation, fears and dangers?

On February 2, 1952, at the age of 25, a young man named Jim Elliot waved goodbye to his parents and boarded a ship for the 18-day trip from San Pedro, California to Quito (Kee-toe), Ecuador, South America.

He and his missionary partner, Pete Fleming, first spent a year in Quito learning to speak Spanish. Then they moved to Shandia (Shan-dee-ah), a small Quichua (Kee-chew-wah) Indian village to take the place of the retiring missionary. Jim and Pete studied hard to learn the language and fit in. Their hard work paid off; in six months, both were speaking Spanish well enough to move to Shandia. When they arrived in Shandia, they also had to learn the speech of the Quichuas.

Three years later many Quichuas had become faithful Christians. Jim now began to feel it was time to tell the Aucas about Jesus.

The Aucas had killed many Quichuas. They had also killed several workers at an oil company drilling site near their territory. The oil company closed the site because everyone was afraid to work there. Jim knew the only way to stop the Aucas from killing was to tell them about Jesus. Jim and the four other Ecuador missionaries began to plan a way to show the Aucas they were friendly.

Nate Saint, a missionary supply pilot, came up with a way to lower a bucket filled with supplies to people on the ground while flying above them. He thought this would be a perfect way to win the trust of the Aucas without putting anyone in danger. They began dropping gifts to the Aucas. They also used an amplifier to speak out friendly Auca phrases. After many months, the Aucas even sent a gift back up in the bucket to the plane. Jim and the other missionaries felt the time had come to meet the Aucas face-to-face.

One day while flying over Auca territory, Nate Saint spotted a beach that looked long enough to land the plane on. He planned to land there and the men would build a tree house to stay safe in until friendly contact could be made.

The missionaries were flown in one-by-one and dropped off on the Auca beach. Nate Saint then flew over the Auca village and called for the Aucas to come to the beach. After four days, an Auca man and two women appeared. It was not easy for them to understand each other since the missionaries only knew a few Auca phrases. They shared a meal with them, and Nate took the man up for a flight in the plane. The missionaries tried to show sincere friendship and asked them to bring others next time.

For the next two days, the missionaries waited for other Aucas to return. Finally, on day six, two Auca women walked out of the jungle. Jim and Pete excitedly jumped in the river and waded over to them. As they got closer, these women did not appear friendly. Jim and Pete almost immediately heard a terrifying cry behind them. As they turned, they saw a group of Auca warriors with their spears raised, ready to throw. Jim Elliot reached for the gun in his pocket. He had to decide instantly if he should use it. But he knew he couldn't. Each of the missionaries had promised they would not kill an Auca who did not know Jesus to save himself from being killed. Within seconds, the Auca warriors threw their spears, killing all the missionaries: Ed McCully, Roger Youderian, Nate Saint, Pete Fleming and Jim Elliot. (For more information on this story, see christianity.com.)

Jim and his friends had a calling to serve the Lord as missionaries. And from the outside, some reading this story of Jim and his companions may think, "What a waste of young lives! Why go in the middle of nowhere to help a people who didn't want to be helped anyways, only to get yourself killed?"

When Jim's body was found with the others, they also found Jim's journal, in which he wrote the following statement that has become the rallying cry for thousands of missionaries who followed their calling after him:

"He is no fool to give up what he cannot keep to gain that which he cannot lose."

Jim's wife, along with the wives of the other young men that died that day, went back to these same Aucas natives and won them over to Jesus. The very ones that took the lives of their husbands, in the end, became brothers in Christ and today, that entire tribe are now followers of Christ.

The man or woman of God who has a calling will always have this sense of self-reliance, who is willing to leave everything, including their families and friends, to seek after this special and unique vocation that the Lord has set aside just for them. It doesn't mean that they find it easy to leave everything behind, but they hear the calling of God and obey it!

In Genesis 12:1, when the Lord told Abram, "Go from your country, your people and your father's household to the land I will show you," I'm sure he had his anxieties and uncertainties of what was about to happen to him. I'm sure when his family asked him where he was going, he honestly had no idea.

Yet because of his self-reliance and trust in the Lord, Abram went. Jim went, and so did Joseph, Moses and David. If you are called, you too will go. You may not know where that road will lead you, you may be called far away from your family and friends, but you will obey the calling because this is your destiny!

LESSONS OF DAVID

The reign of King David lasted for forty years. Seven of those years were in Hebron and 33 years were in Jerusalem.

During that time, David experienced many lessons that we can take away from his life that are useful for the calling. Some of these have already been touched on in other chapters, but I would like to focus on two main ones.

MAKE SURE THOSE CLOSEST TO YOU HAVE THE ANOINTING AS WELL

David had many who were close to him and were influential, both positively and negatively, throughout his life and kingdom. When we think of David's wives, the first name that comes to mind is, of course, Bathsheba. Yet before David ever literally "laid his eyes on her," he had already taken on at least six other wives, all while he ruled in Hebron. David's first wife was Michal, King Saul's daughter.

Although she initially loved David, and was essential in protecting David from her father's murderous plots on several occasions, one thing that we learn about this wife was that she didn't share in her husband's love for the Lord. At one point, she grew tired of David's ways and decided to take (at her father's request) Paltiel, son of Laish, as her illegitimate husband while still technically being married to David.

Michal's true colors are clearly exposed in 2 Samuel 6 when the Bible records King David's successful return of the Ark of the Covenant to Israel after it was taken by the Philistines. David's joy of the Lord's presence was so intense that it says in 2 Samuel 6:14-16:

"Wearing a linen ephod, David was dancing before the Lord with all his might, while he and all Israel were bringing up the Ark of the Lord with shouts and the sound of trumpets. As the Ark of the Lord was entering the City of David, Michal daughter of Saul watched from a window. And when she saw King David leaping and dancing before the Lord, she despised him in her heart."

The reason Michal didn't share in David's joy was because she did not share in his anointing. Rather than celebrating with David that the Ark of the Covenant had returned, all she noticed was that, in her eyes, the King was making a pubic fool of himself.

When it comes to the calling, it is vital that those closest to you, especially your spouse, is a strong advocate of the calling that God has placed upon your life. I am not saying that they are required to be involved in the same capacity as you are, but they should at least have a strong support and appreciation for what you have been called to do. They should be able to weather the spiritual attacks that will be directed not only at you but also at them.

I have seen many ministries hindered or even completely devastated altogether because the spouse was not willing to support and stand with their partner in the calling.

I have always said that the calling of the spouse is just as vital and essential as the one who may be in the spotlight. That partner is just as much called as their spouse. Although they may not be the one whose name is on the door or business card, anyone who is in ministry knows that without their partner's continual support, one's calling would be futile and unsuccessful.

My wife has been my partner in ministry for over 27 years. The truth is, that I would not have made it this long or this far without her help. In fact, I probably wouldn't have written this book without her encouragement.

Lenise and I met when I was in my second year of seminary and she was a freshman. The first time I noticed her was when her dorm was having a "beginning of the year party" in the park adjacent to the back of our school. Since the main foyer of the school faced this park, all the young, single men had a wonderful view of all the new ladies who were new to the school.

Although I noticed her that day, it wasn't until the second semester that I got up the nerve to ask her out on our first date. I was instantly attracted to Lenise's innocence and purity. I found out later, Lenise had given her life to the Lord just a few years earlier, and had been heavily involved in her home mainline church since she was a child.

She had also known since she was a child that she was going to marry a pastor. She just didn't know who, how or when. But she knew it was going to happen. Being raised Anglican, Lenise was committed completely to her local church, involving herself in whatever capacity she was needed, including the choir.

For the next two years, we continued to date. During our summer breaks, we lived so far apart, with me in Thunder Bay and Lenise in Newfoundland. We had to settle with having a long distance relationship in which many love letters were written.

I remember one time when we were talking about our future ministry together, Lenise said to me, "Wherever God leads you, I will always stand by your side."

Neither of us ever forgot those words. From time to time, she had reminded me of them when we were enduring some pretty stressful times in ministry. On August 2, 1991, Lenise and I were married in St. John's, Newfoundland. And although we endured many challenging moments, she kept her word of sticking with me, and I kept my word by providing those challenging times.

Paul mentions in 2 Corinthians 6:14, "Do not be yoked together with unbelievers. For what do righteousness and wickedness have in common?" Paul is not only speaking about marriage relationships with unbelievers, but business and professional relationships as well. I would also like to add the aspect of being unequally yoked in ministry as well.

When a called man or woman of God is looking for a spouse, just because someone is a fellow believer, doesn't mean that they automatically make a good partner for ministry. David's first wife, Michal, was a fellow Jew, even being the King's daughter, a princess! Yet, because she didn't have the same passion for the Lord, their relationship was doomed from the very beginning.

I've said many times that the spouse must be willing to share their partner with the demands that go along with the calling. In leadership, many times one's life can become a very public affair. A spouse must be willing to live in glass houses, knowing that almost every decision that they make may be scrutinized and judged by others.

If a person does not expect this, and they naively believe that marrying someone who has a calling is just like marrying any other believer, they might be in for a bit of a shock.

I remember one time when my wife made the choice to purchase a cleaning business with a family member. A very noble idea, you would think, when you read Proverbs 31! Yet when one family in the church heard about Lenise's endeavor, they became quite upset about this decision. They felt that the pastor's wife should not be involved in such things, because her obligation was to support her husband in ministry.

People are funny that way. On more than one occasion, I have reminded church boards who wanted to hire me that they were not getting a "two for one" deal if they hired me as the pastor. My wife wasn't part of the package.

When we were first starting out in ministry, there was a church that called our home to interview me for their senior pastoral position. Unfortunately, I wasn't home at the time and so the person proceeded to talk with Lenise, saying, "Now before we go any further in the interview with your husband, we need to know one thing. Do you play the organ?"

Lenise's response was totally priceless. She responded in a way that only Lenise could, by saying, "Yes I do, but what does that have to do with my husband? Are you hiring Dan or both of us?"

Needless to say, that church never called us back. That was probably a good thing.

To be the spouse of a called individual is a very unique and inimitable calling all its own. Every called individual, and I repeat, every called individual needs to find a partner in ministry who will support your unique calling. If not, choose, as Paul says in 1 Corinthians 7:32-35, to remain single:

"I would like you to be free from concern. An unmarried man is concerned about the Lord's affairs—how he can please the Lord. But a married man is concerned about the affairs of this world—how he can please his wife—and his interests are divided. An unmarried woman or virgin is concerned about the Lord's affairs: Her aim is to be devoted to the Lord in both body and spirit. But a married woman is concerned about the affairs of this world—how she can please her husband. I am saying this for your own good, not to restrict you, but that you may live in a right way in undivided devotion to the Lord."

Obviously, Paul understood that being single is not for everyone. A point that he strongly makes in 1 Corinthians 7:7 when he says, "celibacy is a gift." As we see in verses 32-35, whenever one is married, there will be demands that will always divide and compete with the responsibilities of the calling.

That is to be expected, and it's not a sin to have this struggle. But if your partner does not understand the responsibilities that ministry demands, that relationship will continue to cause both of you grief and frustration.

If you are called and desire to get married, then be patient, be focused and be discerning. Ask God to show you who that man or woman will be. Accept God's timing. You will need someone who will not only tolerate what you feel you are called to do, but will enhance and compliment your calling.

You need someone who will stand with you through all the ups and downs and will help you not only to survive in ministry, but also to thrive! You need someone who will be your greatest cheerleader and who will stand right by your side.

May I encourage you with this little word of wisdom? Don't focus on finding them. Focus on the work that God has called you to do. When you make your divine calling the focus of your pursuit, and not your future partner, when you least expect it, your partner will suddenly show up! When that happens, you will probably be more shocked than anyone for the wonderful miracle that God has placed before you. And, together you will see the fullness of your calling become a reality!

When speaking about those who are closest to you who support you and your calling, this goes further than just your spouse and helpmate. In your calling, you will need individuals who will not only stand with you, but also will challenge and protect you. People like this are worth their weight in gold, and will be, to coin the words of a Bette Midler song, the "wind beneath your wings" when you need them the most.

Where King Saul's daughter became David's first wife, King Saul's son,

Jonathan, became David's best friend and his greatest ally. This friendship affected and influenced David deeply. When you consider the family name that Johnathan carried, this kinship between David and Jonathan in the natural would seem very unlikely and almost impossible. After all, being King Saul's son, Jonathan was the obvious next heir to the throne! You would think that David would be considered more of a threat to Jonathan's future than an ally.

In 1 Samuel 18:1-4, after David's victory over Goliath, we quickly discover the opposite is true. We see that, "After David had finished talking with Saul, Jonathan became one in spirit with David, and he loved him as himself. From that day Saul kept David with him and did not let him return home to his family. And Jonathan made a covenant with David because he loved him as himself. Jonathan took off the robe he was wearing and gave it to David, along with his tunic, and even his sword, his bow and his belt."

Like David's wife, Michal, Jonathan also protected David from Saul's attacks. The difference between Jonathan and Michal was that Jonathan understood that God's anointing was all over David. This is why you see this commitment to his friendship with David beginning right after the victory over Goliath.

He saw how his father, Saul, cowered from the Philistines, and he saw how David stood up to them. Jonathan understood that David's divine calling to lead Israel was real. He understood that David was being guided by God himself to become King over Israel and therefore, Jonathan was drawn to his authority.

In ministry, because there is an anointing on your life, you will naturally draw people to you who sense God's presence in your life. Don't fight it, don't even downplay it, but never allow it to go to your head. Realize that, especially in our morally-void society, that when there are men and women who obey the appeal to a higher calling, people are naturally drawn to them because of their integrity.

In the positions you may have, you will most naturally become a mentor and inspiration to many. People will come to you for advice on the broadest of topics, even when you may not even be an expert in those areas. Jonathan was drawn to David. He looked up to him like a wiser older brother. We also see from Scripture that in their relationship Jonathan was an inspiration to David as well.

In 1 Samuel 23, we find David fleeing from King Saul's vengeance: "While David was at Horesh in the Desert of Ziph, he learned that Saul had come out to take his life. And Saul's son Jonathan went to David at Horesh and helped him find strength in God. "Don't be afraid," he said. "My father Saul will not lay a hand on you. You will be king over Israel, and I will be second to you. Even my father Saul knows this." The two of them made a covenant before the Lord. Then Jonathan went home, but David remained at Horesh."

Do you see what is happening here? Jonathan is encouraging David. Verse 14 says, "He helped David find his strength." Many years had passed since Samuel told David that he would become King of Israel, and David began to grow discouraged about the King's vengeance on his life.

Jonathan reminded David of his divine calling and says, "My father Saul will not lay a hand on you. You will be king over Israel, and I will be second to you." David's leadership drew loyalty from others. That is the mark of a great leader. As David poured into the lives of others, they in return, willingly poured back into David.

As those called by the Lord, always remember to have people around you who pour into your life. Be careful that those closest to you are not individuals who only know how to take, but are able to give back as well.

Later on in the same chapter of 1 Samuel 23, we are introduced to a group of men that, outside of a few verses, we really don't know very much about. We know that there are around 37 of them and that these "mighty men" (as they were called) were completely loyal to David.

In this story, David and these men are once again fighting the Philistines, who had a stronghold in David's hometown of Bethlehem. In the heat of the battle, while David was exhausted from the fight, I imagine he began to remember a well that he used to drink from as a child, as he says in verse 15, "Oh, that someone would get me a drink of water from the well near the gate of Bethlehem!"

Now understand that David wasn't asking anyone to go and risk their lives to sneak past the Philistine camp and draw him some of that water, he was just reminiscing about how good it would taste at such an exhaustive moment like this.

The words were barely out of his mouth when we read in verse 16-17:

"So the three mighty warriors broke through the Philistine lines, drew water from the well near the gate of Bethlehem and carried it back to David. But he refused to drink it; instead, he poured it out before the Lord. "Far be it from me, Lord, to do this!" he said. "Is it not the blood of men who went at the risk of their lives?" And David would not drink it."

Something tells me that these three men were not shocked to see that their king refused to drink the water that they sacrificed their lives to retrieve. They knew David's heart and as he poured out the water before the Lord, once again, they were reminded why they remained so loyal to this man. It was his love and respect for them that fueled their loyalty, and because of this, they were willing to go so far as to shed their own blood for their king.

As leaders, we must live a life of inspiration to others; living out our faith in such a way that those around us most naturally trust us because we're not afraid of getting our fingers dirty with the rest of them. Going the extra mile to believe in them, as they believe in you.

I have discovered that when you are willing to put aside the façade of being God's perfect person, you will draw like-minded people to you, who will not only become inspired by you, but you yourself will become refreshed by them as well.

If you are longing to have people in your life who will be like a Jonathan to you, like he was to David, ask yourself these questions. "Am I open to correction?" "Am I willing to be real and share my true emotions with those I trust?" "Am I willing to step out of my comfort zone and be stretched in becoming a student all over again?" If the answer is yes, then you will most naturally draw Jonathans in your life.

It is always amazing to me to see how God provides for every need, just like he said he would. About 14 years ago, I was at this place in life where I really needed someone who would be able to provide some fatherly advice. I was pastoring a church in Northern Ontario, Canada. It was a weekday morning and I was spending some time as I regularly did in prayer in the church sanctuary. I was going through some challenges in my ministry where I needed to make some big decisions.

Not having a dad to call on, I began to cry out at the top of my lungs to the Lord, "God I need a dad. I need a dad. God, can you hear me? I need a dad!"

I was so frustrated by the limited mentors in my life, and I desperately wanted someone, anyone, who would just come along side of me and give me some fatherly advice that I was so desperately looking for.

After about an hour of this personal pity party, I got up off my knees, went back to my office and continued on with my day. Yet, inside something felt different. It was almost as if God understood my despair and that an answer to my plea was on the way.

A few weeks later, a gentleman knocked on my office door with a book in his hand. This man was fairly new to our congregation and I honestly didn't know him all that well. He asked if I would consider reading a book about a former pastor who became a messianic rabbi. I politely said that I would, although it wasn't a topic I was all that interested in at the time.

For the next half hour, he explained to me who the author of this book was. He said the author, Alon Barak, was a former pastor who felt led by God

The Calling of David

to go back to his Jewish roots and begin a messianic synagogue in Desert Hot Springs, California. He then added, "Pastor, we have to have him come to our church to teach us about our Jewish roots."

I'll be honest with you. At the time, I really didn't think that having a rabbi in my congregation would fly and I was convinced that church leadership wouldn't be interested in the least.

That evening, because I didn't want to break my promise, I began reading the book. As I read, I found myself not being able to put it down. When I was finished, something incredible was planted in my spirit. After putting the book down, I turned to my wife and said, "I think I need to meet this rabbi guy." She asked me why and I distinctly said, "I honestly don't know, but I just feel that I am supposed to bring this man to our church." Lenise didn't understand why I felt this way. But like always, if it was something that I felt was from the Lord, she was at least open-minded to the idea.

The next day, I dialed the number that was on the back of the book and to my surprise, Alon himself answered the phone. It turned out, that he was at home recovering from surgery after falling off the roof of his synagogue while doing some repairs. A situation that I found out later was a miracle that he survived.

The moment he picked up the phone, I knew that this was a man that I wanted to learn more from. His instant appreciation for my call and desire to get to know me so quickly drew me to him in a way that was difficult to explain to others. It was like we had already been friends for years.

I explained to him that our church wanted him to come up to do some teaching on the Jewish roots of our faith. He said he'd love to come but added, "Before I come up there, you need to come down here to Palm Springs for a Jack Hayford conference. I am part of the planning committee and I would be honored if you'd be my guest." I pondered the thought.... "Hmmm, Palm Springs in December?" It didn't take too much convincing that this was definitely from the Lord and about two months later we were flying south.

At the same time, a wonderful blessing happened in our lives during "Pastor Appreciation Month." A dear friend of ours who attended our church called my wife and said, "I want to bless you and the pastor with a gift to fly you anywhere you guys want to go. Does the pastor have any place in mind?" Without giving it a second thought, Lenise added that I had been talking about wanting to meet this rabbi in California. Without being able to say another word, our friend responded, "Consider it done! Just give me the dates and I'll take care of everything." And with that, our tickets were purchased and we were scheduled to fly to Palm Springs, California.

A few days before we left, we were having a small church prayer meeting at our house. At the end of the meeting, another dear lady who had given me a number of powerful words from the Lord in the past, came up to me and asked if she could pray over my wife and I before we left for our trip. We, of course, gladly accepted the offer, and as she prayed, she gave us a word from the Lord, which explained what this trip would accomplish for us.

She proceeded to say, "This is not just a trip to meet an individual, but we you are about to begin a journey that would change your lives forever." She went on to say, "During this trip you will learn something about your family's history that would be a blessing not only to you, but also to your children." I had no idea what this word would mean, but it would be less than a week that I would find out my answer!

While descending into Palm Springs on the plane, I was so excited about what I was about to experience. I knew it was from the Lord, but I had no idea how. My wife, on the other hand, was much more.... how do I say, "apprehensive" about the whole thing.

As we were preparing to land, she leaned over to me and said, "Now, if I feel at all uncomfortable about this, we're staying at a hotel." We were invited to stay at Alon's personal home, in which she felt a bit awkward doing. I agreed and insured her that everything would be fine.

Once off the plane, I went to the nearest pay phone (pre-cell phone days)

The Calling of David

and called his synagogue. He was so excited that we made it and said that his assistant would be there shortly to pick us up.

"How would I recognize him?" I asked. "Oh, just look for the guy with a black coat and black hat," Alon answered, "you can't miss him!"

Boy was he right. As we stood outside enjoying the warm California air, this vehicle comes pulling up with both front windows rolled down. The stereo was on full blast and Jewish music was playing for all to hear. He got out of his vehicle and asked if I was Dan. I confirmed I was, although for a split second, I thought of denying it. He reaches out his hand to shake mine, "My name is Jonah, I am here to pick you up for Alon."

Well, we loaded up the car and my wife insisted that I take the front seat. I have no idea why. As we were driving, I remember looking back at her and saw this look on her face of absolute confusion. She had no idea what she agreed to be a part of.

I, on the other hand, had never been so pumped! My excitement was still at a ten. I still had no idea why I was there, but for some reason, the Holy Spirit gave me such a peace that this was going to be a total God moment.

After arriving at the synagogue, Lenise and I sat in the foyer waiting as Alon finished off a meeting he was in. Suddenly the door opened and out walked Alon to greet us. In a way that is totally Alon, he completely ignored me, walked over to my apprehensive wife, reaching out both his hands, clasping hers, and said, "And so you're Lenise, I am so honored to meet you." He couldn't have done it any better. He completely melted away her anxiety and from that point on, there was no need for the hotel!

We spent the next week learning amazing things about the Jewish foundation of our Christian faith. Being a former principle of a Christian school, Alon loved to teach, and I loved to learn.

Unlike some other messianic rabbis that I had met over the years who had nothing good to say about the church, Alon was different. He loved the church, and being a former pastor, he had a great respect for fellow pastors and a love and warmth that made you feel appreciated and respected.

Our week in California went incredibly fast. As we were preparing ourselves to go back home, I was still thinking about that prophecy given to us before we left for California. I was supposed to find out something about my past on this trip and still I didn't know what that was.

Before flying out, I remembered from our itinerary that we had an overnight layover in Chicago, which although inconvenient, gave me an opportunity to reconnect with my late father's brother, Helmut Krebs, who lived close by in Southern Michigan. I had not seen him for about 12 years at that time and it would have been a great opportunity to get together. The timing worked for my uncle and his wife and we arranged to meet them at the airport.

While driving on the shuttle bus to the hotel, Helmut turns to me and says, "Did I ever tell you about how your great Opa was also a minister?" "Yes, in fact, you did," I responded. I reminded him that he told me a number of years earlier and that I had been completely surprised at the time, since I never knew that I had any other clergy in my bloodline. He proceeded to say, "Did you ever hear from your dad how your great grandfather protected the Jews from the Nazi's during the war?"

This part of my history I had NO idea about. I was completely stunned when I heard it. "No, Helmut, I've never heard anything about this part of his life!" "Yes," he said, "he was responsible for hiding a number of Jews in the local barns where he lived." Lenise and I just looked at each other dumbfounded.

The prophecy given to us about finding something about our family history came true. I found out that my great-grandfather was not only a fellow pastor, but also protected the Jews during World War II. And when did I find this out? While I was on a trip learning more about the Jewish roots of my faith! What are the chances of this happening? And on top of all that, someone prophesied that this was going to be found out on this trip!

The Calling of David

The moment I arrived home from California, I got on the phone with Alon and told him the incredible revelation. I think he was as stunned as I was and for him to be a part of this incredible moment helped solidify our relationship to this very day, becoming more than just acquaintances, we have become family.

Since that day, we have developed a relationship that has literally changed who I am as a minister. We have prayed together, cried together and fished together. Since the early days of our relationship, he has moved to Israel with his wife and we have stayed in his home in the Holy Land together. I even prayed with him at the Western Wall. How amazing is that? All this, all because I read this man's book.

As a person who is called, God desires to place in your life individuals who will not only support you, but also challenge you.

So many times Alon has lovingly challenged me on some theological viewpoint that I had just accepted as truth because that was what Bible school taught me.

He would ask me a question and I would give him my "pastoral answer." He would respond with something like, "Why do you believe this?" "Where in the Bible does it say that?" And as a patient father, Alon would challenge me to read the Scriptures like it was my first time ever reading them. In doing so, I would discover some incredible nuggets of truth that I never knew were even there.

Once, when I was going through a very dark time in my ministry, I gave him a call to ask for prayer. What I wanted from him and what I got were two very different things. I wanted sympathy, but what I got was a blast of truth.

After telling him how difficult the situation was, Alon responded by saying, "Son, I am so happy for you!" Honestly, that was not what I expected and definitely not what I wanted to hear. He continued by saying, "Son, what you are going through, you need this. This is a test that God is allowing for your eyes to be opened to what is really going on."

Now, many years later, he had no idea how right he really was. He didn't say what I wanted him to say, but he said, in a loving way, what I needed to hear.

Spiritual moms and dads need to do that to you from time to time. Far too many times, the people we have close to us are not strong enough or loving enough to challenge us, or stretch our lives when the advice may hurt a little. If you don't have someone like that in your life, do what I did, ask God for one. Just be ready to learn new things. Be stretched further than you have ever been stretched and grow in ways that you never thought you needed to grow.

Alon has become a grandfather to our children and continues to pray for my family every day and reminds me every time we talk that we are at the top of his prayer list.

My first book, The Beauty of Jesus Revealed in the Feasts, is a direct result of my relationship with Alon. It goes through all the Jewish holidays and explains how Jesus has and will fulfill each of them. I never would have written that book with my co-author, Darlene Schacht, if it weren't for Alon's inspiration. In fact, I dedicated that book to him.

When signing the book for people, I always write at the bottom of the first page, "When you nurture your roots, it feeds your soul." Meaning, when you learn what your Jewish roots are and you are willing to water them, you become a better, more solidified believer in your Christian faith.

So, who have you surrounded yourself with in your life? Do they inspire your thinking? Do they stretch your viewpoint? Do you find yourself always being the teacher and never the student in the relationships closest to you? Then perhaps it's time to stretch yourself to find the Jonathans in your life who will be there to remind you of your anointing and continually challenge you to expand your territory.

David not only had Jonathan in his life, but he also had the prophet,

Nathan. Once David became king, we find that early on in his leadership, he became complacent, or perhaps even a bit arrogant in his role as leader, and began to let down his spiritual guard. It's difficult to understand how such an anointed man of God could stoop to the level of adultery and murder, but stoop he did, to the point that he actually felt that God was able to overlook his guilt without any fear of repercussions. After all, he was God's chosen.

Is it possible to have private sins so hidden that one who has a calling is not even aware that they are there? Something as big as even murder? Every one of us is capable of becoming so focused on the job of ministry that eventually that is all it becomes, a job.

We become numb to our own failures and compromises. We begin to make excuses for seemingly innocent rebellious behavior, which in turn leads, if unchecked, to bigger and more blatant and defiant behavior. We begin to flirt with the idea that holiness is not all that vital in one's life. After all, we all need some down time, from time to time, and shake off our mantle, just for a moment in order to reenergize.

The mantle of your calling must always remain. The moment you jeopardize your integrity, even in the smallest degree, it becomes another weak point that if allowed to go unsupervised will lead you to yet even further failure. You might say, "Well that seems so unfair. After all we're only human, therefore we're bound to make mistakes. We're not Jesus, you know!"

No, Jesus we're not, and mistakes we will make, but as His representatives who carry the mantle of the called, we are not given the luxury of public failure. A Christian man or woman in the church may make the blunder of a moral failure and sin. They will need to confront the sin, confess it and move on from there. They will have their repercussions and criticisms from others. Yet, rarely is their life as affected and compromised as the called one who falls into the same trap.

To the one who "much is given, much is required" (Luke 12:48), the moment we forget that, even for an instant, we threaten the purity of the message that we are trying to represent.

In James 1:14-15, we are reminded that sin never remains small if it is not dealt with, "... each person is tempted when they are dragged away by their own evil desire and enticed. Then, after desire has conceived, it gives birth to sin; and sin, when it is full-grown, gives birth to death."

When David initially saw Bathsheba in 2 Samuel 11, he had no idea that in that moment of sensual desire, everything in his life was about to change. For that moment, he allowed his mantle to fall. In that moment, as I said in Chapter 5, King David was just a man and Bathsheba was just a woman.

But just like anyone who carries the mantle of the called, David wasn't just a man, he was the king. Bathsheba wasn't just a woman, she was the wife of Uriah, a leading commander in David's own army.

When temptation is given over to action, it never just affects the committed and is never satisfied with just a wound. Sin's ultimate outcome, if it goes unchecked, is absolute destruction of everyone affected by it. The death of Bathsheba's husband, Uriah, was a direct result of David's actions. The death of David's first-born son was a direct result of David's actions.

The curse upon his family that the sword would never leave David's hand was a direct result of his actions. Even David's denial from God to build the temple of the Lord was a direct result of David's actions.

How the story would have been so much different if David had just followed the advice of the patriarch, Joseph, and just ran while his temptation was still in its infancy.

In 2 Samuel 12:9-14, the prophet, Nathan, confronts David about his sin:

"Why did you despise the word of the Lord by doing what is evil in his eyes? You struck down Uriah the Hittite with the sword and took his wife to be your own. You killed him with the sword of the Ammonites. Now, therefore, the sword will never depart from your house, because you despised me and took the wife of Uriah the Hittite to be your own.' "This is what the Lord says:

'Out of your own household I am going to bring calamity on you. Before your very eyes I will take your wives and give them to one who is close to you, and he will sleep with your wives in broad daylight. You did it in secret, but I will do this thing in broad daylight before all Israel.' Then David said to Nathan, "I have sinned against the Lord." Nathan replied, "The Lord has taken away your sin. You are not going to die. But because by doing this you have shown utter contempt for the Lord, the son born to you will die."

We read in verse 13 that Nathan encourages David that, "the Lord has taken away your sin." A comforting thought considering his actions. Yet, forgiveness never diminishes the reality of consequences. For the rest of David's life, he would have to live with the reality of what he had done.

Each time he walked by the graves of his newborn son and Uriah, he was constantly reminded of his moral failures. Each time he looked into the eyes of his wife, Bathsheba, he was reminded that he stole her love from another man's arms. Yes, there is always forgiveness, but the consequences, the repercussions, last an entire lifetime.

David's kingdom was spared from complete destruction because David had a Nathan in his life. King Saul had his Nathan through the prophet, Samuel, but the difference between David and Saul was that David was willing to listen to and accept the criticism and advice, where Saul was not.

When confronted about his sin, David responds to Nathan with acknowledgment and acceptance of the consequences of his sin. He says in verse 13, "I have sinned against the Lord."

In Psalm 51:9-12, David puts his sorry to pen as he expresses his mournful heart, pleading with the Lord that God's presence would remain with him.

"Hide your face from my sins and blot out all my iniquity. Create in me a pure heart, O God, and renew a steadfast spirit within me. Do not cast me from your presence or take your Holy Spirit from me. Restore to me the joy of your salvation and grant me a willing spirit to sustain me."

David needed his Nathan in his life to help keep him in line with God's will. Not only that, David needed to obey Nathan's guidance as well.

As the called, you will not survive if you do not seek out and establish Nathans to be a part of your inner circle of influence. You will have to be willing to humble yourself and be willing to be corrected from time to time, no matter how humbling it may seem. No one, no leader, is beyond correction. We all need it because the Lord, "disciplines those he loves," and as His called, His deepest passion for your ministry is complete and utter success.

Your success can only be established when you open yourself up to the wisdom and influence of others, men and women who will help guide you like warning signs along the highway toward your destiny.

PROTECT YOUR FAMILY

Although David was known as Israel's greatest king who was able to bring unity amongst its twelve contentious tribes, I am sure that the one thing that grieved David's heart the most was his inability to unify his own family.

Afflicted by murder, jealousy, incest, revenge and attempted coups — when reading about what was taking place within David's own family unit, it wouldn't be difficult to think that you were reading a novel of some factitious family melodrama.

Being married to at least eight wives, he fathered 19 sons. With this, David created an environment for himself that invited dissension and discord, which only escalated when he was unwilling to bring order to the rebellion.

At the time of his rooftop moment with Bathsheba, David had already taken on several wives and had numerous children. Despite his "at home" responsibilities, David still found it within his carnal nature to long for one more relationship, even if she belonged to another man.

It seemed that although David was able to sing so eloquently, and write such incredible Psalms like, "the Lord is my shepherd" (Psalm 23), David had a difficult time being the shepherd in his own household.

As fathers, I discovered that our children really don't care what we verbally teach them, unless they see that we actually live it out before them.

I remember one evening when my children were little, we were saying our bedtime prayers. My oldest daughter, Taylor, spoke up and said, "Daddy, did you ever drink beer?" Now, never seeing their father drink alcohol of any kind, each of my children resolved in themselves that beer was bad, because Daddy never touched it. One time, my son who was about five years old at the time, resolutely said to his mother, "I'm never going to drink beer because it's water with bad germs in it!"

Being a teetotaler was a decision that I personally made when I was 19 years old. Putting my testimony above my freedom to drink alcohol was a decision that I made for myself in order to not allow my "weaker brother to stumble," according to 1 Corinthians 8 and Romans 14. It was a decision for me, and I am definitely not using this book as a platform or soapbox to say that drinking is necessarily wrong for you. It was a decision that I needed to make for myself and was done to satisfy my personal convictions.

Anyhow, my kids never saw their dad or mom drink and so when Taylor asked me if I ever drank alcohol, in her mind as a child, it was like asking Daddy, "Did you ever rob a bank?"

In their innocence, they could never imagine Daddy doing anything that was that "bad." So when I had to admit that there was a time when I did drink, you should have heard the gasps in that bedroom that night as my children tried to grasp the reality of my honest confession. My youngest sweetheart, Aliyah, was only a couple of years old at the time, so she really had no clue what "depraved sin" her daddy had just confessed to. But for Taylor and Jordan, I will never forget the looks on their little faces as they tried to take in what their daddy just admitted to. For the next hour and all the next day, all they kept on saying was "Daddy drank beer. Daddy drank beer!"

I understand that this story may be a somewhat elementary and silly example, but it brings home the point. Our decisions, whether they happened many years ago or are choices we are making at the present time, always impact our children in a negative or positive way.

If my children were to decide that alcohol was going to be an acceptable part of their lives or not, perhaps the choices that I made for myself many years ago might be part of their deciding factor in the end.

David had no idea how his misguided decisions would eventually affect those closest to him. If he did, I'm sure he would have made different choices from those he did.

As his children learned about the foolish choices that their father chose to make, it subsequently taught them that such behavior was not only acceptable, but also actually beneficial. That their stepmother, Bathsheba, was part of their family only because Dad chose to murder her first husband to get what he wanted.

Think about it, we teach by our actions and even when our misdeeds are forgiven before the Lord, to our children, they are signs of approval that such behavior is worth repeating.

As mentioned earlier, after the prophet, Nathan, confronts David about his sin, he did say that David's sin was forgiven, but that there would still be consequences for what he had done:

"Now, therefore, the sword will never depart from your house, because you despised me and took the wife of Uriah the Hittite to be your own. This is what the Lord says: 'Out of your own household I am going to bring calamity on you. Before your very eyes I will take your wives and give them to one who is close to you, and he will sleep with your wives in broad daylight. You did it in secret, but I will do this thing in broad daylight before all Israel.'"

For the called, it will always be your number one responsibility to protect your family's character and reputation. Each wrong decision that is made is

The Calling of David

never an act that affects just our lives, but can cause long-lasting emotional damage to those we love the most.

I have heard and seen the many horror stories of what the "ministry" has done to pastors' families. Many "PKs" or "MKs" (pastor's kids, missionaries kids) choose to never dart the doors of the church again or even consider ministry for themselves. This may be the result of humiliating or frustrating moments that they had to endure because they were part of the family of the "anointed one."

Ministry on its own will have pressures and expectations placed upon one's family even when personal failure is not part of the equation. People will have false assumptions on how your perfect family is to behave and interact. This alone can cause stress and anxiety in your home.

For those of us who have chosen, or should I say God has chosen, to live in the glass house of ministry, we must always be sensitive to the Holy Spirit's leading in order to avoid unnecessary harm. The Holy Spirit will warn us of dangers and temptations that the enemy will try to throw in our pathway.

It didn't take long after Nathan's prophecy to David to begin to be played out in real life. In the next chapter, following Nathan's rebuke on David (2 Samuel 13), we find that David's son, Amnon, becomes obsessed with his half-sister, Tamar, who was Absalom's sister. After receiving his father's blessing for Tamar to go to Amnon and prepare a meal for him, Amnon quickly takes advantage of her and rapes his sister and then immediately banishes her from his home.

After being defiled, we read in verses 19-22, "Tamar put ashes on her head and tore the ornate robe she was wearing. She put her hands on her head and went away, weeping aloud as she went. Her brother, Absalom, said to her, "Has that Amnon, your brother, been with you? Be quiet for now, my sister; he is your brother. Don't take this thing to heart." And Tamar lived in her brother Absalom's house, a desolate woman. When King David heard all this, he was furious. And Absalom never said a word to Amnon, either good or bad; he hated Amnon because he had disgraced his sister Tamar."

Not only was Absalom infuriated with what Amnon had done to his sister, but also it says that, "when King David heard all this, he was furious." Rightfully so, considering that he gave his blessing for Tamar to meet with Amnon in the first place. The problem is in what David does afterwards. David does nothing!

Where David should have intervened immediately and protected his daughter's reputation, the Bible is completely silent about his response. Silent because there was no response given.

In the following verses, it says that Absalom waited two years before he chose to take things into his own hands and avenge his sister's rape. Why two years? I personally believe that Absalom was waiting on his father to intervene and deal with Amnon. In Absalom's mind, David chose to turn a blind eye.

Why did David act this way? Was he unconcerned about his daughter's well-being? Did he feel it wasn't his place to step in as the father and confront Amnon's misbehavior?

I believe that the answer to this question goes right back to David's own failings. What he saw in Amnon's misbehavior was what he saw in himself. David refused to confront his son because his son did what he himself did just a few years earlier.

Perhaps David even felt that Amnon's behavior was directly influenced by David's own misguided behavior with Bathsheba. How could he chastise someone for emulating what he himself was guilty of committing?

Despite David being able to so eloquently speak of God's grace and forgiveness in the Psalms, I believe that there was still a part of David that, during the last half of his life, could not completely forgive himself and come to grips with what he did.

It is the same with us in ministry. How many are so good at teaching and preaching on God's grace and forgiveness, yet deep within them, they fall short in fully embracing it for themselves.

In your ministry, you will have moments of failure. And when I say failure, this may not even necessarily be speaking of personal sin. It could be something like a wrong financial decision for your organization, a ministry project that went array, or a conflict with staff. Yet, because you are the person in leadership, the focus of that failure comes back to you, or you feel it should because you are the leader, and because of this, you carry an element of shame.

Learn it early on in ministry, or better yet, before you even start ministry, that you are infallible and will make mistakes as a leader. This doesn't justify it, but it is a reality that you have to face. David needed to take his own advice found in Psalm 32:1-2, "Blessed is the one whose transgressions are forgiven, whose sins are covered. Blessed is the one whose sin the Lord does not count against them and in whose spirit is no deceit."

Shame is an incredible handicap that will ruin any leader in ministry. There are men and women who are called of the Lord, yet shame that stems from failures before, or even worse, during their ministry, keeps them from fully stepping out in what God wants them to do.

Shame will always hold you back from going to the next level in your calling. It's a tactic of the enemy to try to neuter any further success in your divine calling.

The King David that we read about after his initial encounter with Bathsheba is a very different man than from his youth. We no longer see him being the young David who defied Goliath and the entire Philistine army on behalf of the God of Israel.

Although he continued to be used by God, and succeeded in his role as king, inside David had changed. His purity was tarnished and in the end, the extent of his success was diminished. John Maxwell puts it this way in his commentary of 2 Samuel 13:

By this point, David's leadership has shrunk to a mere shadow of its former self. Note the changes in David's leadership:

1. He no longer works proactively, but passively interacts with those close to him (vs 30-31);
2. He no longer expresses joy, but is full of grief and mourning (vs 31);
3. He no longer acts in his convictions, but buys into rationalizations about his loss (vs 32-33; 39);
4. He no longer solves problems, but licks his wounds (vs 34-36);
5. He no longer pursues his desires, but remains paralyzed regarding Absalom (vs 39).

Shame is a terrible bedfellow. It will rob you of all joy, passion and vision, but because God's calling is still on you, like David, God will still use you, but now your confidence has been shaken.

And the truth is, unless you confront it once and for all, it will drastically weaken your calling. Worse yet, it will emotionally affect those closest to you.

Shame also has a way of confusing your ability to know God's will. While fleeing for his life from his son Absalom in 2 Samuel 16:7-8, David is approached by a man named Shimei, who was from the same clan as King Saul, David's predecessor. The Bible says that Shimei began to throw stones at David and his band of followers while crying out:

"Get out, get out, you murderer, you scoundrel! The Lord has repaid you for all the blood you shed in the household of Saul, in whose place you have reigned. The Lord has given the kingdom into the hands of your son Absalom. You have come to ruin because you are a murderer!"

As this man heaps vile curses on King David, notice the accusation that he is making. He tells David that the reason why his life is in danger is because God is punishing him. And why? Because, of all the blood that was shed on the household of former King Saul. To top it off, he calls David a murderer, twice.

Oh, how the devil knows where to thrust the dagger, doesn't he? When we are struggling with failure, when we are questioning where God is, it's those times that the enemy tries to get us in our most vulnerable state. In response, David's answer reveals to us just how confused and disillusioned he was about God's presence in his life.

After David's nephew, Abishai, asks permission to execute this vile offender for what he said to the king, David responds in verses 10-11 by saying, "What does this have to do with you, you sons of Zeruiah? If he is cursing because the Lord said to him, 'Curse David,' who can ask, 'Why do you do this?'" Now listen to what he says next, "Leave him alone, let him curse, for the Lord has told him to."

Can you imagine? At this point, David is so disillusioned, so disheartened, that he contemplates the thought that perhaps Shimei may actually be right in what he is saying. David thinks perhaps this man is actually speaking on behalf of God when saying these vile things to him. That maybe the Lord was actually punishing David for Saul's removal from the throne and that David was a murderer!

Oh, there's that word again. Murderer. In David's shame, that memory continually haunted him for years, and now, on the run, it felt that God had removed him once and for all from his throne.

If, as a leader, you begin to question the direction of God's will, and begin to wonder if God is for you or working against you, you are in a danger of losing your influence on others.

The enemy may not call you a murderer, but he will know what accusation will aggravate you the most. Perhaps he will call you a failure, a hypocrite, a fraud or even too unintelligent to be a spiritual leader. Whatever adjective he will try to use to describe your reason for shame, the enemy knows what notes to play in your mind. If your mind is in this place, whether you verbalize your concerns and fears or not, people will sense it. They will feel your anxiety and discern your lack of confidence.

People that follow you as their leader need to know that God is working through you. If you are not even sure of this for yourself, guaranteed, they will begin to look elsewhere for inspiration and direction. John Maxwell says in his book, <u>The 15 Invaluable Laws of Growth</u>, "If you place a small value on yourself, rest assured the world will not raise the price."

This is exactly what happed with Absalom. Earlier on in the story in 2 Samuel 13, I believe that Absalom grew frustrated when he felt his father was turning a blind eye to Amnon raping his half-sister, Tamar. After waiting two years without any response from the king, Absalom had enough.

There is no doubt that Absalom's devotion towards his father had died many years before this situation with Amnon occurred. Yet, I believe that if Absalom had seen in his father just a glimpse of a fire for righteousness and justice towards dealing with Amnon, perhaps the outcome would have been different. If Absalom would have seen in his father what Jonathan saw years earlier in David when David confronted Goliath, perhaps David could have won back his son's loyalty.

This was not the case. Because Absalom saw only weakness, and an unwillingness to do the right thing, he in turn considered his father to be a failure and became convinced that he could become a better king than David.

From this point on, after killing his brother, Amnon, Absalom became determined to overthrow his father's kingdom. He began conspiring the people against David and was successful in convincing a large portion of David's fighting men to turn against his father and even forced the king and the rest of his family to flee for their lives.

In the end, David's loyalists began to overtake Absalom's rebel army. While fleeing on his mule, Absalom got his infamous hair caught in the branches of a large oak tree and while hanging by his locks in midair, David's commander, Joab, killed the king's own son.

The Bible says that when David heard about Absalom's death, he mourned deeply. Part of the reason he did so was because he knew in his heart that his own failure as a father and a king helped create the dissident that Absalom became.

The biggest failure that any called individual can do towards their family is lose the passion of your calling. When we lose our passion, when we refuse to confront our failures, we become weak and insecure in who we are and what we have been called to do.

Even those closest to us, like Absalom with King David, will begin to lose their respect for us and become cynical to every aspect of the calling.

Many children of called individuals, who themselves no longer serve the Lord, say that their parent/s were different in private than they were in their public ministry. In other words, they were hypocrites.

When you live in shame, when you begin to lose your passion, you might be able to fool the masses for a while like David did; but your family will always be able to see right through you.

Do you want to protect your family from the onslaughts of ministry? Do you want them to actually be proud of what their mother or father do for a living? Then never lose your passion! Be open about your fears and failures, yet constantly seek to be refilled and re-empowered with the Holy Spirit.

You will never be perfect, but may those closest to you always see you as a person who strives for integrity and holiness. May they know you as a person that doesn't show it by being legalistic and authoritative, but rather as one who walks in humility and integrity and inspiring others to do likewise.

LEGACY OF DAVID

When speaking about King David's lineage, out of any monarchy that reigned at any time in human history, it is only King David's throne that is spoken of in Scripture that promises to be an everlasting throne. During the future millennial reign, the Bible tells us that Jesus himself will sit on the throne of David (Psalm 132:11-12; Isaiah 9:7).

In Luke 1:32-33, the angel Gabriel told Mary that the baby within her would be "... great and will be called the Son of the Most High. The Lord God will give him the throne of his father David, and he will reign over Jacob's descendants forever; his kingdom will never end." Therefore, when it comes to David's legacy, we can wholeheartedly say that it will be a lasting one.

Even the heavenly temple, which will be re-established when Christ returns, originated with King David desiring to build a more permanent structure, rather than the portable tabernacle that was in use until then.

He was responsible for amassing great stockpiles of resources and material that were designated to build the first temple. He established the guidelines for the priestly duties within the temple so that all its rituals would be conducted in a proper and holy manner.

It was David who gave the legacy of establishing worship within the temple, amassing over four thousand priests who were put in place to be the temples' choirs and musicians (1 Chronicles 23). The very concept of singing worship music in synagogues and churches originated when David (the harp player) established these parameters as a regular part of the sacraments in the first temple.

Hundreds, if not thousands, of worship songs have been written and inspired based upon the inspirations of David's original Psalms, which have influenced the Jewish people and the Newer Testament church for thousands of years.

Yet, because he was a king who had blood on his hands, like Moses who was forbidden to enter into the Promised Land, David was forbidden to oversee the construction of the first temple. This privilege would be passed down to his son, Solomon, once David had died. Once built, the first temple would last for over 300 years, until the Babylonians destroyed

The Calling of David

it in 586 BC (2 Samuel 7; 1 Chronicles 17).

Of course, the greatest legacy of King David would be that it was from his family line that the promised Messiah Jesus (Yeshua) himself would come. That the coming Messiah would even choose to be born in the same town, Bethlehem, as King David, shows that God had a special place and an important role for this red-haired young man. Despite his failures in life, despite his misguided moments, the Lord still looked upon David as "A man after God's own heart."

For the called, I pray that King David's legacy would be an encouragement for each and every one of you. The calling that the Lord has ordained for your life was there before you were even born. David knew this when he wrote in Psalm 139:14-16:

"For you created my inmost being; you knit me together in my mother's womb. I praise you because I am fearfully and wonderfully made; your works are wonderful, I know that full well. My frame was not hidden from you when I was made in the secret place, when I was woven together in the depths of the earth. Your eyes saw my unformed body; all the days ordained for me were written in your book before one of them came to be."

This reality for David's preordained calling was there his entire life. It did not waver, despite his misguided decisions. Unlike King Saul before him, David had a repentant heart. He acknowledged his sin and the Lord restored him. Yes, there were consequences for his sin, but he remained king until his dying day and his love for God never waned, despite his inability to fully forgive himself.

In his last moments of life, David speaks a blessing over his son, Solomon, who is about to be crowned as the new King of Israel. 1 Kings 2:2-4 says:

"I am about to go the way of all the earth," he said. "So be strong, act like a man, and observe what the Lord your God requires: Walk in obedience to him, and keep his decrees and commands, his laws and regulations, as written in the Law of Moses. Do this so that you may prosper in all you do and wherever you go that the Lord may keep his promise to me: 'If your descendants watch how they live, and if they walk faithfully before me with all their heart and soul, you will never fail to have a successor on the throne of Israel.'"

I love the first part of his statement. Not only does David challenge Solomon to keep God's Mosaic laws and commandments, with the promise of a long enduring reign, but he begins with something that ties all these truths together. He says, "So be strong, act like a man!"

When one is getting older, they begin to look back upon their life and think of things that they should have done differently. I believe that David was doing a bit of this at that moment. He realized that in the later years of his life, because of his failures, because of his shame, David became insecure and even intimidated by those he ruled over.

Because of these shortcomings, he became weak in the eyes of some of his own people, and worse yet, in the eyes of some of his own family. His love for God had never changed, but his confidence had changed from when he was a young man.

As his dying eyes looked into the face of this bright, handsome young man who was about to become king, his first words were "Be strong, act like a man." What did David mean by this? Its meaning was much more than a man-to-man giving his son a shot in the arm, saying, "Be a man, stay tough." What David was saying to Solomon was, "Son, don't become weak as I did." Stay true to your convictions, stay true to your morals and stay true to God. Be a man!

As leaders, as those who are called, we need to stay true to our convictions, our morals and our God. Never slip from what you believe in. The convictions and passions that made you choose the difficult choice of ministry in the first place must never waver and needs to actually mature and grow stronger over time.

The Calling of David

If you have failed in your ministry, if you have made decisions that you now regret, this does not mean that your calling has been removed from you. Oh, as I said already, there may be consequences to face, but that does not mean that God is finished with you, as long as you are open to correction.

Allow King David to come forward in time and say to you at this moment, "Be strong, act like a man (woman) of God. Observe what the Lord your God requires. Walk in obedience to Him and keep His decrees and commands. Do this so that you may prosper in all you do and wherever you go."

John Maxwell says; "All leaders make mistakes. This is part of life. Successful leaders recognize their error, learn from them and work to correct their fault."

You will be a successful leader in ministry if, when you fail, you learn from those failures and move on. In doing so, you will find yourself becoming an inspiration and mentor to other fallible people who themselves are on this road of the calling.

CHAPTER 8

DON'T FORGET YOUR FIRST LOVE

Throughout this book, when referring to the term "calling," I have done my best to avoid referring to the more common aspects of church oversight and leadership (i.e., pastor, evangelist, missionary, etc.). The calling to ministry has really nothing to do with what type of ministry you go into. It is more about what kind of leader you are as you carry this mantle.

If you are called, it is because God has placed an internal, spiritual seal on you, and has set you apart for a very special purpose. A calling is not necessarily better or more important than other believers, but rather something that is different, unique and specific. It has been created by the Creator just for you.

Considering the patriarchs from the previous chapters, was Moses still in God's will when he was taking care of his father-in-law's sheep for 40 years? Was Joseph still in God's will when he was the slave of Potiphar or lying in prison? Was David still considered to be God's anointed one when he was fleeing for his life from King Saul and from his son, Absalom?

The obvious answer to these questions is a resounding, unequivocal YES AND AMEN! Our outward circumstances and environments and situations can never, and will never, remove that divine calling that God has placed within you before you were born.

Even before you were following the Lord, that anointing and calling was on you. No matter what place in your life you may presently find yourself in, your calling is still there, just as strong and just as anointed!

As long as you are not in a state of rebellion, like Jonah boarding a ship heading for Tarshish in the exact opposite direction of God's will, as long as you are still trusting the Lord and have a passion to be obedient to His will, you can rest assured you are right where you are supposed to be.

Even though your present chapter, your present surroundings, and yes, even your present career may not be where you thought your ministry would have taken you, rest assured, it is all a part of God's bigger plan for your calling.

However, I need to stress, don't settle there. As Joseph still held onto his integrity in Potifer's house, as he still remained strong to his convictions while in prison, you too need to hold tight and keep pressing into God. Your present situation is only a small part of the journey of your calling.

There are many in ministry who find themselves remaining in their present calling, and perhaps have been there for years because they believe that it is what they were ordained and destined to do. Even the thought of leaving that line of ministry could never even be considered or entertained because they believe that they would instantly be walking away from God's calling on their life and away from His blessing.

May I encourage you that this is far from the truth. Never hold onto your present ministry as if this is all that you were ordained to do. If what you are presently doing is distancing you from your life-long ordained calling, maybe it's time for a new chapter to be opened that could absolutely change everything.

In Revelation 2:4, Jesus says to the church of Ephesus, "But I have *this* against you, that you have left your first love" (NASB). Just like this ancient Ephesian church, the person who is called can also be in danger of forgetting their first love, of losing the very passion that inspired them to consider ministry in the first place. If this is you, maybe it's time to revisit your initial passion that led you down this path years earlier.

Oh, you may be a few years older, you might even be a little wiser, but you need to ask yourself, "Does my passion for ministry still drive me? Do I still wake up in the morning with new visions and desires that God has given me for my ministerial work?" If you can't honestly say "yes," then perhaps it's time for some changes. Perhaps it's time to allow the Lord to give you some new dreams and exciting visions.

I don't care how old you may be, and it doesn't matter how long you have been in ministry, if your passion and zest for the calling has waned, it's time to ask yourself why.

Psalm 37:4 tells us, "Delight yourself in the Lord and he will give you the desires of your heart."

A major problem for many of us in ministry, whether we realize it or not, is that we really don't even know what the "desires of our heart" are anymore. And if we do, it might seem too long since we felt them, where they become nothing more than a distant memory from a bygone era of youthful innocence. Now, after living in the trenches of "real" ministry for years, you've resolved to believe that the reality of working for Jesus is nothing but "blood, sweat and tears." Therefore, any thought of "enjoying" the Lord's work is thought of as only for the immature, naive and inexperienced.

"GET OUT"

After 26 years of full-time ministry within the same denomination and district, I found myself reaching a wall that I couldn't describe at the time or even explain. The denomination that I had been with my entire ministry was all I knew. I couldn't imagine doing anything else.

I thought that this was the group that the Lord put me under and this would be the organization that would one day retire me out to pasture with a plaque and pension in hand!

In the last three years of my full-time pastoral ministry, the church had gone through some difficult times that caused incredible stress for me and for my family. Determined to persevere through it all, once some challenges seemed to be behind us, we rolled up our sleeves and began a renovations project that was well overdue in our 40 year-old facility.

Upon completion, it was something to behold. We now had a building that we could be proud of and on opening Sunday, city council members were there to help our congregation and staff cut the ribbon. It was beautiful, it was special, and I was so proud to be their pastor.

It was during a sabbatical shortly after the renovations were completed that I had a very clear and vivid dream from the Lord, which changed my life and future forever.

In this dream, my wife and I are standing in an incredibly beautiful barn. In this barn, I didn't observe any animals, but I did notice that it was made from large stripped, varnished logs.

As Lenise and I stood there observing this building, I suddenly heard one of the exposed roof trusses cracking and beginning to give way. I said to my wife, "Stay here, I'll go fix it." I quickly grabbed a ladder, climbed up and begin nailing the damaged truss back in place.

I went back to my wife and said, "It's all okay now, I fixed the problem." Suddenly, I heard and saw another truss begin to crack and give way. Again, I said to my wife, "Wait here, I'll go fix it." I climbed the ladder and once again did my best to nail it back into place.

It seemed like hours, but for most of the dream, all I was doing was running from one weakened truss to another trying to fix this roof that seemed to be about to cave in. Finally, after I thought it was all fixed, I came back to my wife where she was standing and with both us looking up at this ceiling that I worked so hard to repair, I turned to her and said in an exhausted tone, "Okay, now it's all fixed."

All of a sudden a beam fell from the ceiling and landed right beside us, just missing my wife. At that moment, we both heard a loud voice (a voice to this day I swear was audible), which cried out to us, "Get out!"

It was then that Lenise and I found ourselves outside of the barn looking up at the roof. The roof was being torn off in such a way that it looked like a tornado. But it wasn't a storm. It was the hand of God removing the roof. God was fixing it from the outside; the only real way a roof can be properly fixed.

It was then that I heard the voice say to me, "You can't fix this, I have to." It was at this moment that I woke up. Now, if you are a pastor, and I was a betting man, I would bet my last nickel that you know exactly what God was saying in this dream.

I had spent 11 years of my ministry trying to fix something that only God could. I went from one issue to another saying, "I can fix this," yet through all of this, I had no idea of how it was affecting my family and causing me to lose my passion.

This congregation had many good things going for it. It had wonderful ministries that were reaching their community. But to truly change the spiritual DNA of this particular congregation was something only God could do, and I wasn't him. I, nor any pastor, could do what needed to be done. They needed a divine intervention, which they had to desire and plead to God for.

It was through this dream that God showed me something about myself that I failed to realize, although it was glaring at me straight in my face. I had lost the passion, the desires of my heart within my calling. It was time for a change, and if I didn't make that change soon, it would affect my immediate family (beam falling right beside my wife).

The Lord was saying, "Get out." Not in a stern, harsh manner, but as a loving father who cared for the well-being of His children. He longed for me to get back to the desires of my heart, to my first love.

I couldn't see this reality through all the clutter of ministry. But the Lord knew exactly what I needed, and on that night, he made it very vivid and clear to both my wife and I that things were about to abruptly change.

Within months of that dream, I had resigned from my church and stepped out in faith into the great unknown. Being an unemployed pastor is not an easy place to be when it comes to your resume, especially when it was all you did for 26 years.

I was "shocked" to discover that companies don't care that I worked as a laborer in a factory THIRTY-THREE YEARS AGO, way back in 1986! Surely that had to count for something!

As I am writing this book, I am 52 years of age. Since that step of faith, I must admit it hasn't been easy. Nothing worthwhile ever is. Despite the risks, I have witnessed with amazement how the Lord has been slowly peeling back the onion and revealing some of His bigger dreams for my future.

Like Joseph, there were long forgotten dreams that the Lord had revealed to me in my youth that I am beginning to see blossom into beautiful completeness.

Although the road of ministry has changed for me, the calling has not. Yes, it can be stressful gazing into the unknown, not knowing what lies ahead. Yet, if in your heart you are convinced that it is the Lord's will, what else really matters?

Take that step. Take that risk! You never want to look back after all is said and done wishing that your faith had been strong enough to make the changes when you had the chance.

CONCLUSION

If the Lord has called you to ministry, you are on a journey that will forever alter your life. As was told to Queen Esther long ago, you have been chosen to impact your world "for such a time as this."

There will never be another "you" in this world. God created you uniquely and perfectly for the task he has set before you. I remember my mom telling me when I was in my early 20's that she asked the Lord, "Are you going to use my son like Keith Green." In response, she said the Lord clearly said to her, "I will use Dan in the calling I have set out for HIM!" I wasn't called to be another "Keith Green," but was called to be the Daniel Krebs that He ordained for me to be.

In your calling, never aim to be like someone else that you admire. Joseph, Moses and David were very different from each other in personality, passion and ability, yet each of them was called to their own unique task set out for them by the Lord.

In your calling, there will be times when the pressures of ministry will weigh heavily upon you and you will want to plead with the Lord to remove the heaviness of this mantle. There will also be times that you will wonder, "Why was I so blessed? Out of all people, why was I chosen by the Lord to have this incredible honor and blessing of being set apart for His work?"

Always remember that it is your calling. It is your mantle, uniquely prepared and blessed by God just for you. Protect it, honor it and never forget who chose you to wear it.

Your calling was placed upon you long before you knew about it and long before you were a part of this world. But despite the fact that you were set apart by the Lord for a unique purpose, always know that the direction of your distinct calling is completely up to you.

When we read the story of creation, we find that after God created everything so perfect and uniquely beautiful, He said to Adam in Genesis 1:28, "Be fruitful and increase in number; fill the earth and subdue it. Rule over the fish in the sea and the birds in the sky and over every living creature that moves on the ground."

In Genesis 2:20, it says, "So the man gave names to all the livestock, the birds in the sky and all the wild animals." In both of these verses, we see God's calling to Adam. God gave Adam the free will to subdue the earth and to name and rule over the animals.

In other words, God gave Adam a blank canvas and told him to paint it as he pleased. God didn't say, "Now that this world is created, this is what I want to do with it." No. God left that part of things completely up to Adam.

In many ways, you need to look at your calling in the same manner. Although your calling to ministry has been set apart by the Lord, and there are some very unique directions that the Lord desires for you to go, God has given you a roadmap and He has allowed you the free will to choose which road to take in order to get to that destination.

I remember a time in my life when I had a choice of three different ministries that were offering me a position at the same time.

Two of them were typical church staff positions and one was in a parachurch ministry where I would be working with men with addictions. All three seemed very interesting to me and I knew that whatever choice I made, I would be completely fulfilled in that type of ministry.

My problem was that I wanted to know HIS will in this situation. I was praying and saying, "God, show me your will. Which ministry would you prefer?"

Conclusion

I remember the morning that He gave me His answer. As I was having my morning prayer time while the rest of my family was still in bed, I heard the Lord so clearly say to me, "Dan, you choose. Whatever direction you desire to go, I will bless it."

I remember feeling so relieved by this revelation. I felt that the pressure of accidentally choosing the wrong ministry was no longer a concern. Soon after that, I made the choice and the Lord sent me and my young family into a new direction.

If Moses decided that day to bring his sheep to a different pasture that was far away from burning bush, if David decided to go into town the day Samuel showed up to Jesse's home, if Joseph decided not to visit his brothers that fateful day when they sold him into slavery, would their destinies have been lost?

The obvious answer to that question is, of course not. God would have used another means, other opportunities, to get their attention and finally in line with His will for them.

Even when we make mistakes, even when we are running from the calling, God will always have an incredible way of bringing us back in line with His ultimate will.

I encourage you to do what you will be teaching others, to trust the Lord. Know His Word and rely upon the Holy Spirit's leading. Step out in faith, even if you fail. It's only failure if you don't learn a powerful lesson from it.

God will guide you, He will keep you, He will sustain you. And in the end, He will use you for His will. Your impact on others will live on long after your voice is finally silenced. God's Word working through you is eternal. I challenge you to show me any profession that has that type of impact!

> "In the sight of God, who gives life to everything, and of Christ Jesus, who while testifying before Pontius Pilate made the good confession, I charge you to keep this command without spot or blame until the appearing of our Lord Jesus Christ, which God will bring about in his own time—God, the blessed and only Ruler, the King of kings and Lord of lords, who alone is immortal and who lives in unapproachable light, whom no one has seen or can see. To him be honor and might forever. Amen."
>
> **1 Timothy 6:13-16**

Made in the USA
Middletown, DE
30 May 2019